BARGELLO:
AN
EXPLOSION
IN
COLOR

BARGELLO: AN EXPLOSION IN COLOR

Margaret Boyles

MACMILLAN PUBLISHING CO., INC.
NEW YORK
COLLIER MACMILLAN PUBLISHERS
LONDON

To Barry and Hope with love

Macmillan Publishing Co., Inc.
866 Third Avenue, New York, N.Y. 10022
Collier-Macmillan Canada Ltd.

Library of Congress Catalog Card Number: 73-2753

First Printing 1974

Printed in the United States of America

ACKNOWLEDGMENTS

My most grateful thanks are extended to all my friends at the Columbia-Minerva Corporation for their interest in this book and their generous contribution of all the yarns and canvas used in preparation of the Bargello illustrations.

Also, fondest thanks to my editor who made writing this book such an exciting and rewarding project.

Margaret Boyles

PREFACE

Bargello is beautiful, repeated geometric design; long, quick-to-work vertical stitches; colors vibrant and contemporary or softly traditional; patterns that adapt readily to many uses.

Bargello is not new but old. No one is sure where or when it originated. This embroidery is found in many countries and is known by many names—flame stitch, Hungarian stitch or Point de Hongrie, Florentine embroidery, and even Bargello. Today, all are gathered together under the one name, Bargello.

Museums are rich with old, well-preserved Bargello, which serves as testimony to the fact that this embroidery has long been a favorite. Some of the most-used and loved designs of the past, such as the flame stitch, remain among the favorites today. Updated by color and used creatively these old designs adapt to modern needs as if they had been newly originated.

Bargello depends heavily on color to achieve its unique designs. Color changes or changes in the direction of shading of color can so alter a design that it is sometimes difficult to recognize that the variations are one design. Many Bargello designs achieve a kind of optical illusion created by the color shading that is used. If the sequence of shading is changed the depth of the illusion often disappears. A switch from shades of one color to rows of contrasting color will accent another aspect of the design and greatly alter its feeling. When color experiments are begun it seems that there is no limit to the variations of design.

And so this book is produced in color—color vibrant or soft, color contrasting or analogous, color monochromatic or multihued. Containing a collection of beautiful and varied designs that can be adapted to a multitude of uses, this book provides an understanding of the way color works in Bargello design and explains the mechanics of Bargello design. Only with a thorough knowledge of the materials and working techniques of Bargello can beautiful and creative designs be produced. Bargello is pure joy—joy in the creative pleasure that comes only from producing with your own hands something that is both beautiful and useful.

Margaret Boyles

CONTENTS

1
MATERIALS

Bargello is a special form of needlepoint that uses the same materials employed in other forms of needlepoint. However, since Bargello is a very specialized type of canvas embroidery there are bits of information about materials that will be interesting and helpful.

The single most expensive ingredient that will go into your Bargello is your own time. With this in mind, you should shop for materials and buy only those that will make the best use of your time. Good yarn and fine canvas will contribute greatly to the enjoyment of working on a project. Cheap materials are definitely more difficult to use and may completely discourage a beginning needleworker. Don't be trapped into trying a poorly constructed kit to find out if you are going to like Bargello. With poor materials chances are that you will be very unhappy, both with the work and with the finished results. No matter how beautifully worked, a piece can never be worth more than the materials that it contains.

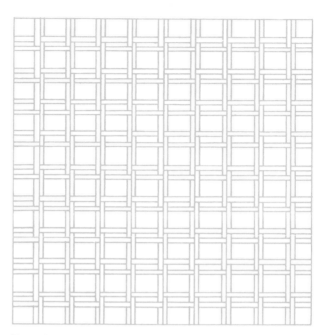

Penelope canvas

Mono canvas

Canvas

Like needlepoint, the foundation of Bargello is canvas. Made from either cotton or linen threads, this familiar fabric has an open weave of mesh or squares into which the stitches are worked. There are two very distinctly different weaves in canvas. Both kinds are shown in the accompanying drawing. Either type of canvas is suited to Bargello embroidery; the choice is one of personal preference rather than one based on suitability.

Shown at the top of the drawing is Penelope or double canvas. This canvas has a very distinctive weave. Close inspection reveals that the warp and weft threads are in pairs and that each intersection of canvas is formed by four threads. These threads interlock at each crossing in a manner that makes a very stable canvas. Note also that the vertical pairs of threads are placed close to each other whereas a small space separates the horizontal threads. Because of this weave, Penelope does have a definite "up and down grain." It is best to form the habit of always working the piece with the selvadge edges forming the sides because the stitches will fit the canvas better.

The piece of canvas shown at the bottom of the drawing is mono canvas, which also is sometimes referred to as uni, single, or congress canvas. As its name would indicate, mono canvas is woven so that one horizontal and one vertical thread cross at each intersection. This results in an open weave that is very easy to see and less confusing to the beginner. This feature probably accounts in part for the increasing popularity of this canvas. Even when the size of the canvas is small, the mesh openings are easy to see, making this the easiest canvas on which to work.

Since the threads of the mono canvas merely cross and do not interlock, this canvas does require quite a large amount of sizing to hold the threads in place. This is not a disadvantage unless the sizing is excessive and irritating to the hands. When the canvas is rolled in the hand properly for working, the normal sizing is not objectionable.

There is a new development in canvas weaves that is not shown because it would look exactly like the mono. This one is called interlocking mono. Like Penelope, the warp and weft threads are in pairs but are so closely entwined that they give the appearance of being one. However, at each intersection the threads interlock to form a very firm crossing. This gives interlocking mono canvas all the advantages of both of the other canvases—a good firm weave plus an open, easy-to-see mesh.

All three types of canvas are woven in either white or ecru. Color will not affect the quality of the canvas in any way, but it should be considered in view of the colors that will be worked on the canvas. If most of the colors will be light the natural choice should be white. For a design using darker shades of colors the ecru canvas would be better. Any small portions of canvas threads that may show at the top of the Bargello stitches will be less obvious if there is less contrast between the colors of the yarn and the color of the canvas.

Canvas is available in many sizes, the size being determined by the number of mesh per inch. This number is the name given to the size. Thus number 5 canvas will require five stitches to cover one linear inch, number 10 will need ten stitches and so on.

The sizes most suitable to Bargello are numbers 10, 12, 13, and 14. However, special effects may warrant the use of rug canvas—number 5—or one of the finer canvases usually reserved for petit point. Bargello stitches worked in bold colors on rug canvas with heavy rug yarns work up swiftly into smashing accents, whereas the tiny stitches on petit point canvas can be as delicate as the finest embroidery. Choose the size of your canvas keeping in mind the finished effect that you want. All will be beautiful, but some will be more appropriate to a given situation than others.

You should choose canvas very carefully and reject any that has an excess of irregularities. Threads that have many thicker sections will cause uneven stitches. Knots are weak spots that may break when the canvas is stretched in blocking. The canvas should feel smooth to the hand—smooth, round threads will make the embroidery so much more pleasant to work and will speed completion.

Yarn

One of the greatest pleasures in working Bargello is watching the design grow as the colors interact with each other. The large and growing popularity of all needlework has led manufacturers to market yarns in a variety never before known. Finding the colors and precise yarn for any project is now a pleasure instead of a seemingly endless search. Persons who are far from a city need only to consult a catalog, those in town have a choice of many specialty shops. Informed salespeople are provided in most shops to assist those unsure of their needs. In short, shopping for the materials for a Bargello project is pleasant and choosing yarn will be exciting. Families of colors with as many as six shades are offered to make the delicate shadings of Bargello possible. Bright contemporary colors that almost sing have been added to traditional shades so that there are many selections to appeal to every taste.

Persian yarns are among the most versatile and widely used needlepoint yarns. These yarns are especially adaptable to Bargello. Because they are three-ply yarns with a light twist, they can be used for various sizes of canvas by separating the ply. Used as they come from the skein, they cover well on number 10 canvas. Two strands of the three-ply yarn are fine for numbers 12, 13, and 14 canvas. This yarn has a softness that spreads out and covers well.

Despite their softness, Persian yarns are sufficiently long-wearing to be practical for most Bargello projects, even chair seats and other upholstery. Most have been moth-proofed and are colorfast. Learn to read the labels when you shop for yarn. Most manufacturers have gone to great trouble to put all the important characteristics of a specific yarn on the label. Space on the label is small, and so you can be sure that the information you find there is pertinent.

One important fact that you will find on the yarn label is whether the yarn has a dye lot. If it does, it is better to purchase enough to complete a project at one time. Dye lots do vary slightly, and though in many Bargello pieces these variations can be concealed, it is so much simpler not to have to worry about it.

The designs in this book have all been worked with Columbia-Minerva Needlepoint and Crewel Yarn. This is one of the new breed of Persian-type yarns that is particularly good for Bargello. To begin with there is a glorious range of colors that includes subtle shadings of the important colors. The yarn has a soft, light twist that gives it very good covering qualities, which are necessary to Bargello. It is packed in a convenient one-half-ounce pull skein that makes it possible to cut exactly the length needed. The small-size skein is also convenient when many colors are going to be needed as in many Bargello designs. This yarn is worth looking for—your favorite shop or department store probably has it in stock.

The familiar and traditional tapestry yarn is not well adapted to Bargello. Although it is an excellent needlepoint yarn, it has a very tight twist that does not allow the yarn to "fluff out" and cover the canvas when the stitch is one of the upright ones so common to Bargello. Save it for other projects in which its special wearing qualities are needed.

Hand-knitting yarns can be used for Bargello, but when deciding to use these yarns keep in mind that they were designed with special qualities built in. One of the most important qualities of these is softness, and this same softness makes them rather impractical for use on any project that will get hard wear. Avoid their use in pillows, chair seats, and upholstery, but investigate their use for fashion accessories, pictures, and other small decorative items. Remember also that an extremely soft yarn will "pill" and tend to look shabby very quickly.

There are other possibilities for materials with which to work Bargello. It is always fun to find and use a material that no one has considered. These effects can be very unusual and can turn even a basically simple pattern into something special. Usually it is better to combine these "found" materials with yarn rather than work an entire piece with them, but that again will have to be determined by the desired finished effect.

It is not necessary to be tied to convention if you wish to experiment with new materials for Bargello. There are many possibilities. Strips of leather and suede are especially good with rug yarn on large canvas. What about a few gleaming rows of satin tubing? This is an expensive material, but its effect can be so great that only a small amount is needed. Many types of cording are now available for macramé and other projects formed with knots. Some of these may be good. Fine ribbon can be worked into a design. Don't forget some of the hand-knitting yarns which have been spun with textures and colors that will be sure to be great additions.

Cotton embroidery floss can be worked into Bargello with very attractive results. The smooth strands of thread look almost like silk and add luster to the pattern. The fineness of the strands makes it necessary to use more than one strand for most canvases, but if the threads are kept from twisting they can be combined very smoothly. If as you work the thread wants to twist on top of the work, take the tip of the needle and straighten out the stitch. Working with embroidery floss is not as easy as working with yarn because of this tendency to twist, therefore the use is best limited to small areas for accents.

Embroidery floss has been incorporated into some of the worked designs in this book. Where it was used it has been noted. In a few instances embroidery floss made of pure silk has also been used. This thread is very hard to find and is expensive, but there is nothing to compare to the luster that silk imparts.

Needles

The needle used for Bargello is the tapestry needle. It has an elongated eye, a tapered body, and a blunt point. Needles range in size from a very small 24 to a large 13. For most Bargello projects the sizes covered in the chart will be correct. It is very important that the size of the needle be exactly right. The eye must be large enough to carry the yarn through the canvas easily, but it must not be so large that it forces the canvas threads apart unnecessarily. On the other hand, if the needle is too small it may cause the yarn to wear out. Needle and canvas must fit each other exactly, therefore it is wise to have a selection of various sizes on hand and find the one that is right for every project. Below are some helpful guidelines.

number 5 canvas—size 13 needle
number 10 canvas—size 18 needle
number 12 canvas—size 18 or 19 needle
number 14 canvas—size 20 needle

Scissors, Thimble, and Frames

A pair of good embroidery scissors with smooth tapered blades that are sharp to the very tips is not a luxury. Reserve them for embroidery only, and when you keep them with your needlepoint be sure to keep them in a little case so that those sharp points do not accidentally damage your work.

There are some people who feel that any work done with a needle requires a thimble. These people are very uncomfortable without their thimble and should most certainly use it for all needlepoint, including Bargello. However, there are also many people who find it clumsy to use a thimble and can not become accustomed to using one. No matter. Beautiful needlepoint can be done with or without a thimble. To be comfortable is the important thing.

Whenever any type of needlepoint is discussed, there is always much talk about frames, to use one or not. It is always a big question. There are advantages both to using a frame and to not using one. Like the use of the thimble, it is a decision that the individual embroiderer will have to make.

Bargello does not stretch the canvas out of shape and really does not require the use of a frame. To put it on a frame makes it less portable. Also when the canvas is stretched on the frame, it is necessary to work with one hand above and one hand below the frame. Each stitch is then two operations rather than one. The use of the frame, however, will maintain the canvas in its original new condition with all the threads straight and true. Rolling the canvas in the hands will soften the sizing and may cause some slippage of the threads. This can be overcome if care is taken not to unnecessarily fold or mistreat the canvas while it is being worked.

And so you see each method has its advantages and disadvantages. It is probably best to try using a frame and then to try working without one before making a decision. Enjoy your needlepoint and work in the manner that makes it easiest to produce beautiful work.

Kits

The packaged needlepoint kit as we know it today is really a product of modern times. It is a convenience that should not be overlooked either by the beginner or the expert. A good kit will be well designed and contain all the materials needed to finish a given project. The design more than likely will have been planned by a leading artist and expert in the field, and there is no need to shop further for additional materials.

Look at these offerings before you make your next purchase. You will be pleasantly surprised at the variety available and at the savings in money you can make. Kits are generally a very good buy because you need to pay only for the exact amounts of yarn needed—there's no need to buy full skeins of every color. If the design needs only a few yards of a color, that is all you pay for. It is really a good concept.

Do shop carefully for a kit. Check the package to make certain that you can see all the contents. A good kit will be packaged so that all materials are clearly visible. With a well-packaged kit you have the same opportunities to examine the canvas and yarn as if you were buying separate items.

CANVAS 1

2
THE
STITCHES

The Bargello Stitch

For the most part Bargello is worked with one stitch—the upright Gobelin—placed on the canvas in a way that is so characteristic of the work that it is called the Bargello stitch.

The stitch is a simple upright one that lies parallel to the vertical threads of the canvas and varies in length from two to six threads. Generally, the Bargello patterns dictate that the stitches be placed in steps moving up and down in rows across the canvas. This is the Bargello stitch arrangement.

These same stitches placed side by side in rows across the canvas are called the upright Gobelin stitch. These are not two different stitches, they are only the same stitch arranged differently on the canvas thus creating a different pattern on the canvas. The upright

Gobelin stitch will create a strong horizontal pattern with a slightly raised effect. See the top illustration on page 10.

When the stitches are placed in steps as in the Bargello stitch, variations in the length of the stitch and in the height of the step can change the shape of a pattern drastically. If, for instance, as shown in the middle section of page 10, all the stitches are worked over four threads in steps one thread above the last, the line is one of compact stitches forming a series of peaks. This is known as a 4–1 step. To work down the slope the stitches are placed one thread below the bottom of the last.

If the stitches are kept the same length but placed two threads above the last stitch, as in the second example in the photograph, the result is a much steeper peak. This is called a 4–2 step. The number of stitches in a peak in the lower illustration is the same as that above, but the line is finer and the peak higher.

The same variations hold true with stitches two- and six-threads long. These and other variations of stitch placement will be discussed further in the chapter "Understanding Bargello Design."

Practice the Bargello stitch by following the charts and working the stitches in the order indicated by the numbers. Three charts are shown as a guide to the three different placements of stitches.

The charts show only one row of stitches to avoid confusion. The lower row of stitches illustrating the 4–2 step does, however, show part of the second row. Stitches are placed immediately under the stitches of the row above with the top of the new stitches occupying the same mesh as the bottom of the stitches above.

As you practice the stitch, learn not to pull the yarn too tightly— let it relax and "fluff out" to cover the canvas. If in the beginning you see the canvas between the stitches, the problem probably is that the tension is too tight. This is a common occurrence with beginners, but it can be easily overcome with a little practice.

Decorative Stitches for Variety

Although Bargello is worked predominantly in the one stitch— the Bargello stitch—other needlepoint stitches can be successfully incorporated. The stitches that will fit together with the Bargello stitch are generally those that are also worked upright on the canvas. The

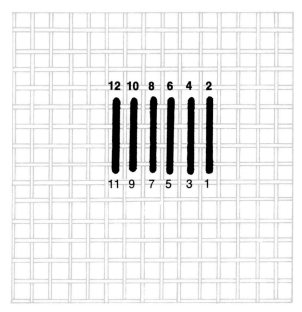

Upright Gobelin

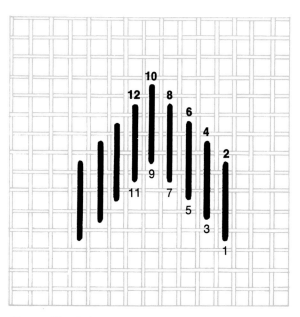

Bargello 4-1

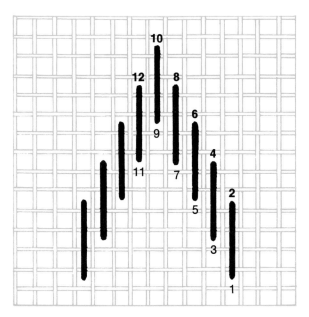

Bargello 4-2

Tent stitch
CANVAS 2

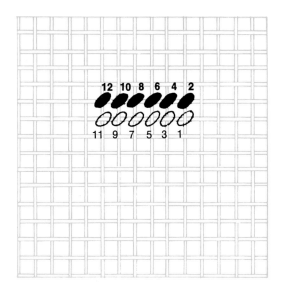

Continental stitch

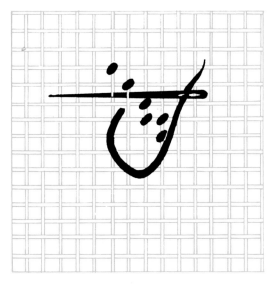

Basketweave stitch

basic tent stitch and three of the upright stitches are diagrammed for those who would like to experiment with additional stitches. Also charted is the diamond eyelet stitch, which makes an interesting center for some of the diamond patterns. Even though this selection is limited, the needleworker should feel free to use any stitches that will fulfill the need for textural interest and at the same time adequately cover the canvas.

Readers who would like a broader selection of stitches would enjoy *Needlepoint Stitchery* by Margaret Boyles. This book presents a new and creative approach to the whole spectrum of canvas embroidery and includes a wide range of stitches. Many of the ideas in the book will be applicable to Bargello and will open new vistas to the needlepointer.

Each of the stitches discussed in this chapter is shown in a plate of a worked sample and in a working diagram. The charts are a unique feature of this book. Notice that some of the numbers are in lightface type while others are in boldface type. The lighter numbers indicate that the needle is coming up out of the canvas, the darker ones show the needle going down into the work. Thus at a glance one sees the path of the needle.

Work the stitches by first following the diagrams exactly, but then experiment and try reversing the stitching direction. The simple fact is that some people are more comfortable stitching in one direction than in the other. The difference in stitching direction will not affect the look of the stitches or the quantities of yarn needed.

When working any of the needlepoint stitches that lie upright on the canvas, care should be taken not to pull the yarn too tightly. These stitches merely lie over the canvas threads and if worked too tightly will reveal the threads underneath.

The Tent Stitch

The tent stitch is the basic needlepoint stitch and probably familiar to all. It is included here as one of the stitches that will combine successfully with Bargello stitches. An area worked in tent stitch will be flatter than the surrounding Bargello stitches and therefore an effective accent.

Both the continental and basketweave stitching methods have been diagrammed. Use the one most convenient for you. To be sure that all the canvas is covered in the areas where the Bargello and tent stitches meet, work the tent stitches right up to the very edge of the long Bargello stitches and place stitches under the edge of the last row. Do this by slightly lifting the Bargello stitches along the edge and placing the continental stitches underneath.

The Parisian Stitch

The Parisian stitch is a group of three stitches—two short and one long—arranged in a neat little pattern that is good either as part of a design or as a background for a bold border. The upright stitches will mesh perfectly with the Bargello stitch creating no problem where the two meet.

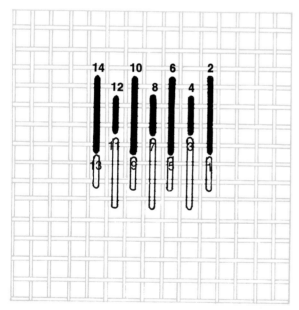

Parisian stitch

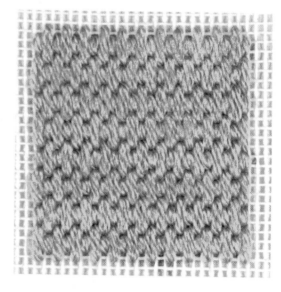

CANVAS 3

The Hungarian Stitch

The Hungarian stitch adapts very well to Bargello. The neat little stitches are a good background for a border or can be used to work all or part of a pattern. In the blue and white design shown here, the entire design has been worked in Hungarian stitches. An interesting variation would be to work only half the diamonds in Hungarian and the remainder in Bargello.

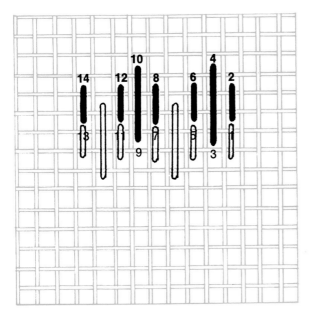

Hungarian stitch

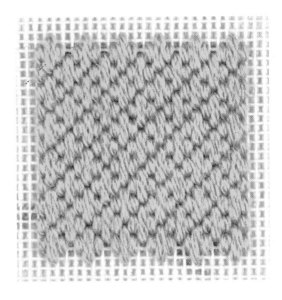

CANVAS 4

The Brick Stitch

The brick stitch is the upright Gobelin stitch again; this time arranged so that the stitches are alternately two threads up and two down, which creates the "brick" pattern. For this reason it will also fit very well into a Bargello pattern. This is an easy, quick stitch to work, and it forms a textured but unobtrusive background for busy patterns. The gold argyle-plaid design shown below has been worked with the entire background in brick stitches.

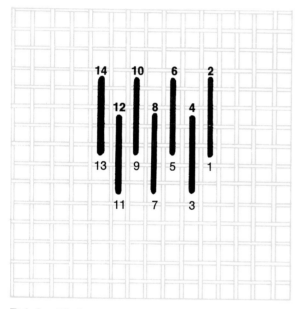

Brick stitch

CANVAS 5

The Diamond Eyelet Stitch

The diamond is a constantly recurring part of Bargello designs, and the diamond eyelet stitch is a natural for filling in those areas when a little different center is wanted. It is wise when using this stitch to make all stitches in the same sequence so that all end alike. Only the odd numbered stitches are noted in the diagram because all stitches go down into the canvas in the center mesh.

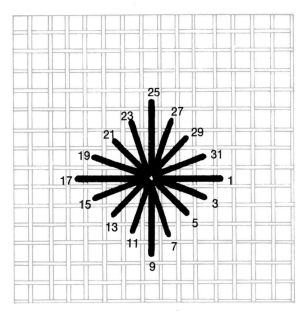

Diamond Eyelet stitch

CANVAS 6

3
BARGELLO TIPS

Bargello is a form of needlepoint, and a working knowledge of the basics of needlepoint will be helpful but is not absolutely essential. Added to the instructions given with the stitches themselves, the following tips will enable even a beginner to carry out the beautiful Bargello patterns.

Measure carefully the item that you are going to cover. Needlepoint cannot be blocked out to a larger size when completed. On the other hand it is a waste of both time and materials to make a piece larger than necessary.

Before beginning to work, tape the cut edges of the canvas with masking tape or sew folded bias tape into place over the edges. The tape will not only keep the canvas from fraying but will also keep the yarn from snagging on the stiff cut threads. Other types of tapes—cellophane and adhesive—are not practical for binding canvas. They do not stick well enough and sometimes become sticky and messy after much handling.

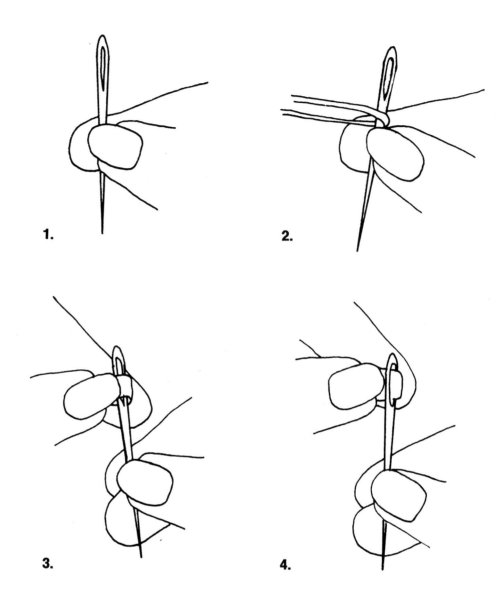

Method 1:
1. Hold the needle between the thumb and forefinger of your right hand with the eye of the needle facing you.
2. Fold the yarn across the needle and pull it tightly to form a fold.
3. Continue to hold the fold tightly with the left hand and withdraw the needle gently.
4. Force the fold through the eye of the needle.

1.

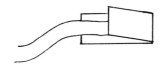

2.

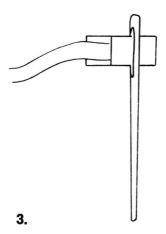

3.

Method 2:
1. Cut a small piece of paper narrow enough to pass through the eye of the needle and about an inch long.
2. Fold the paper in half as shown in the drawing and place the cut end of yarn in the fold.
3. Pass the folded end of the paper through the eye of the needle and the yarn will be carried through easily.

When a project is planned, a two-inch border of canvas that will not be worked should be allowed on all sides of a piece. This is not, as it might seem at first, a waste of canvas but a very functional border that helps maintain the shape of the canvas and makes blocking easier. Do not hinder yourself with a skimpy border. Some small projects like eyeglass cases or pincushions will require only a one-inch border, but most will need the full two inches.

If the piece you are going to make is of irregular shape, mark the outline on the canvas and work only the needed portion, but keep the canvas either square or rectangular until after it has been blocked. The square-shaped canvas will retain its shape better during the working and will be easier to handle in blocking.

If you draw lines on the canvas, use either a waterproof marker or a strand of yarn. Ink may bleed into yarn. Pencil marks will rub off, losing the markings and perhaps staining light-colored yarns.

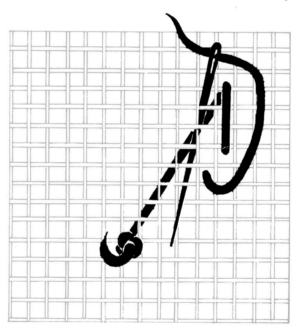

Waste knot

Knots are usually not used in needlepoint, but the waste knot, which is removed when its purpose has been served, is very good for solving the problem of fastening the first few loose Bargello stitches.

Make a knot in the end of the yarn. From the right side of the canvas go down into a mesh about an inch from where the first stitch will be, leaving the knot on the top. Bring the needle up and start stitching. When the knot begins to interfere with the stitches, clip it off. The little end will fall through to the wrong side and there will be no evidence that a knot was used.

The waste knot is used only for the very first stitch on the canvas. The ends of subsequent strands of yarn are fastened by working them into stitches already existing on the wrong side of the canvas.

Anchor the first stitch on a new canvas with a waste knot. This knot will hold the first few stitches neatly in place when you start the first row. Other methods of securing the first stitch are not very good here because the Bargello stitches are long and loose. Begin and end other strands of yarn by weaving them back into stitches on the back of the work. Work the ends back a little farther than for other needlepoint stitches because the Bargello stitch is loose on the back. Clip the ends short enough so they do not tangle and pull through to the front side of the work. When several colors are being used it is very annoying to have fuzzy little ends of another color pull through and become mixed into the stitches being worked.

Since the Bargello stitches are long, they will use up the yarn quickly. For this reason it is possible to use a little longer strand of yarn than is generally used for other needlepoint stitches. A length of fifteen to sixteen inches is usually enough. More would be awkward to use and would cause the yarn to wear thin before it was used up.

Learn to work the Bargello stitches with a light, even tension. The stitches lie upright on the canvas and must be worked loose enough for the yarn to fluff out and cover the canvas well. If small portions of the threads show at the tops of the stitches or the threads are visible between the stitches, the tension is probably too tight.

To look best, the Bargello stitches should lie flat on the canvas with no twisting of the yarn on the front side. Guide the yarn with your fingers so that a perfect stitch is formed. If the yarn twists as it comes up out of the canvas, loosen the stitch with the tip of the needle and straighten the yarn with your left hand as you tighten the stitch again. Smooth, even stitches enhance the beauty of Bargello designs.

If, as you work, you notice the yarn twisting, hold the canvas up and let the needle swing free. It will unwind itself. Never work with the yarn when it has become twisted. It will not cover the canvas, and the stitches will be uneven.

Many Bargello designs depend heavily on delicate shadings of color. Very often these shadings are difficult to differentiate under artificial light. To avoid making mistakes by using the wrong shade, it is helpful to mark the skeins in a manner that will identify the shades for you. In these particular designs it is usually wise to work all of a given shade before going on to the next.

There is no set rule about which portion of a Bargello design must be worked first. Each particular design will have to be examined before this decision can be made. All designs should be centered on the canvas and worked from the center line. Designs that are merely a series of continuous lines will naturally have to be worked one row at a time. Some designs are composed of one continuous line that will establish a pattern of small motifs made up of broken lines. These are usually best handled by setting the pattern over the entire canvas with the continuous lines, then going back to fill in the motifs one color or shade at a time. This method gets all the counting out of the way in the beginning and is the ideal way in which to work. There are times when it is just too difficult to wait to see what the design is going to be like, and when this happens there is nothing wrong with completing a few motifs to satisfy this urge. This will make the embroidery more interesting, and after all that is the most important consideration.

Centering the Design and Placing the First Row

It is very important that Bargello designs be centered on the canvas. Form the habit of placing the patterns on the canvas correctly, and you will never be disappointed with an unbalanced design. The process is so simple that it becomes automatic after one experience.

Divide the canvas into quarters as shown in the photograph. Use a waterproof marker or a strand of yarn to make the two perpendicular lines through the center of the canvas. The first row is worked from the intersection of the two lines to the left edge following the chosen chart for placement of stitches. At the left edge, end the yarn and go back to the center of the piece. Finish the row by working out from the center to the right edge. This will complete the first row. It will now be possible to work the subsequent rows all the way across the canvas in a continuous row. Only the first row needs to be divided to center the design.

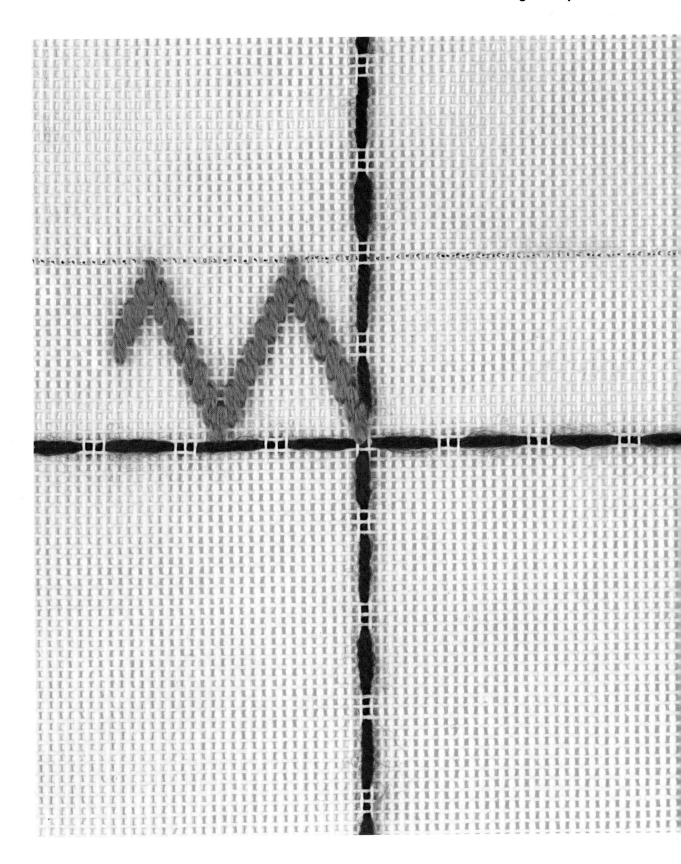

Work the bottom half of the canvas first. At the completion of this section, turn the canvas completely around so that the bottom is now the top. Complete the remaining section being careful to keep the colors in the proper sequence.

Very often it is true that the first row of a Bargello pattern will establish the design and that all other rows merely follow. It is very important that this first row now be counted carefully, for a mistake here will carry through into the rows following. A simple device that will help beginners to place the first row correctly is the additional line shown in the photograph. The flame pattern was used as an uncomplicated first choice, but the principle will apply to most of the "easy" patterns.

Carefully count and place the stitches of the first peak. Draw a line on the canvas following the thread that the top stitch touches. Continue to work the row, counting the stitches from the chart and checking as you go to make sure that the top stitch of each peak touches the same thread as marked. If you have made a counting error, it will be apparent that the mistake is in the last few stitches made, and it can be corrected easily.

In some designs where the first row dips below the center line—like the one on page 44—a second line drawn along the line of the lower edge of the curve would be helpful. This would act as another checkpoint for the first row.

After you have worked a few Bargello designs, the lines are no longer necessary as you will be able to run your finger along the threads to check yourself as you stitch. This habit of constantly checking will save much ripping.

At the edges of a piece there will always be portions of motifs that will not be complete. Finish the edges into a straight line by working only the portion of the design that would lie within the line. At the bottom and the top it will be necessary to make adjustments in the lengths of some stitches in order to work out a straight edge. When you reach this point it will be easy to see just what is needed.

Try to keep your canvas in the best possible condition while you are working on it. If the sizing holding the threads in place is broken, the threads will slip out of alignment and the stitches worked over them will not be even. The sizing will deteriorate if the canvas is folded and refolded. You should avoid this by rolling the canvas in your hand when you work, and roll it rather than fold it when putting it away.

Mistakes should be ripped out and corrected as soon as they are discovered. Fortunately Bargello stitches are easy to rip. If you are careful, you can insert the tip of the embroidery scissors under the stitches and clip them. The loose stitches can then be easily picked out from the wrong side. If you prefer, or if there are only a few stitches to be removed, they can be picked out one at a time with the tip of the needle. Do not choose this method of removal in order to reuse the yarn. It is better to discard this yarn and begin with new yarn rather than to try to use the removed yarn again. It is usually worn and thin and will not cover the canvas well.

Care must be taken when cutting out stitches so as not to accidentally damage the canvas. However, if you do mistakenly cut a canvas thread or discover a broken one, it can be mended. If only one thread is damaged, rip out the needlepoint stitches around it. Take a thread from the edge of the canvas and weave it into the cut area for a distance of five threads on either side of the cut. Duplicate the weave of the canvas as closely as possible. When the Bargello stitches are replaced over the mend it will be invisible.

A larger damaged area will have to be repaired with a patch. The canvas for the patch must match the damaged canvas in weave exactly. The patch should be cut several mesh larger than the hole and should be basted into place matching the mesh of the two pieces. The Bargello stitches are then worked through the double thickness where the patch overlaps. This mend will be strong and invisible.

The best and most important advice that can be included in a book on Bargello is to work carefully, giving each stitch special attention so that it will lie perfectly and be part of a series of smooth even stitches. The surface of Bargello is beautiful when graceful stitches combine with vibrant colors to create this very special embroidery.

4
UNDERSTANDING BARGELLO DESIGNS

The two factors primarily responsible for Bargello's appeal are color and the repetition of regular geometric design. When the designs are taken apart and examined, it becomes apparent that careful use of color is the key to the complexity of many designs. Without color most designs would be simple lines of stitches marching across the canvas. The interplay of colors in the design can vary the overall effect according to the way the colors are placed. The importance of this effect of color cannot be overemphasized. Color use is often vital to a design as in an optical illusion where a reversal of the direction of shading can obliterate all depth and render the design meaningless. Careful shading can tie a group of lines together into a whole, while the use of contrasting colors for those same lines would set each line out in definite contrast to its neighbors. The possibilities for color change in a Bargello design are many and varied—some are good; others should be discarded. Experiments with color are very interesting and should be tried by any embroiderer interested in Bargello design.

For these experiments a sampler is a very valuable tool. When actually worked on the canvas, the changes caused by color rearrangement are often very dramatic. On the sampler many color arrangements can be worked out and saved as a reference for future work. This color "magic" becomes very fascinating, and the sampler very often becomes an attractive piece in itself.

Naturally, all the elements of Bargello—color, stitch length and step, texture of yarn, canvas size, and the basic lines themselves— enter into the overall picture to create the beautiful Bargello designs. It is often surprising when a design is dissected to find that the basic lines forming the design are really very simple. It is usually the other elements that combine to present the complicated finished appearance. In fact these basic lines are usually so logical in their development that one wonders about the mystery surrounding Bargello design. A breakdown of the basic lines also shows the progression from the easiest flame pattern to the more complicated motifs.

The favorite old flame pattern, so much used and loved, is the simplest of all Bargello designs. Variations on this line are endless, and careful coloring can combine with these to adapt the design to a multitude of uses. This probably accounts in part for the popularity

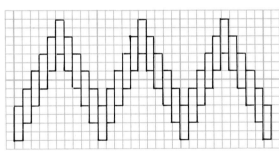

1.

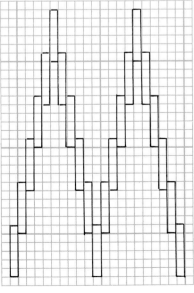

2.

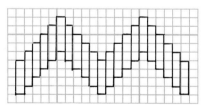

3.

of the flame pattern through the ages.

Sketch 1 shows the flame, small in scale, worked in a 4–2 step in regular peaks six stitches high. This is Bargello reduced to its simplest form. The peaks can be worked any number of stitches high according to the scale of design needed.

Changing the step, as in sketch 2, alters the appearance of the line. The peak is still six stitches high, but the step was changed to a 4–1 resulting in a less steep slope and a more compact line. A change to the 6–1 step, as in sketch 3, will produce the dramatically steep, jagged peaks for an entirely opposite effect.

Sketches 1 through 3 show the flame pattern worked so that all peaks are the same number of stitches high resulting in rows of regular "flames." The versatility of this line will allow the peaks to be worked in varying heights in a single row for a more interesting design. This opens up the possibilities for endless variations beginning with those suggested by sketches 4 and 5. The giant flame shown on page 38 is a development of a line of this type. One very large peak has been centered between two small ones—a very simple line pattern, but the addition of color brings it to life and makes it a very striking design.

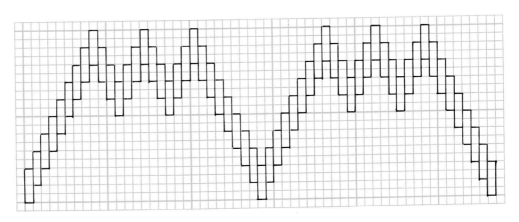

5.

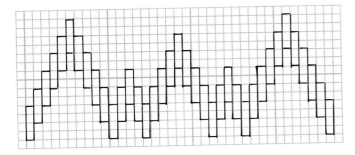

4.

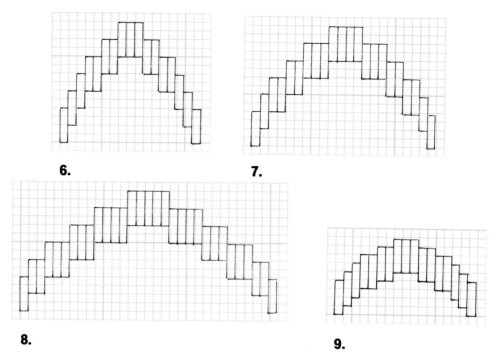

6.   **7.**

8.   **9.**

The curved line is the basic flame pattern with stitches added in groups to create the rounded shape. The greater the number of stitches added along the curve, the more rounded the line will be, as evidenced in the sketches. The smallest number of stitches has been added to sketch 6 progressing upward in sketch 7 to the gently rounded arch of sketch 8. These three sketches were worked in a 4–2 step. Sketch 9 shows the change when the arrangement of stitches is the same as that in sketch 6 but the step is changed to 4–1. There is a more compact line of stitches and a less accentuated arch.

When one row of the regular flame is reversed against another exactly like it, the result is a series of diamonds. (See sketch 10.) Changes in the flame pattern will dictate the sizes and the shapes of the diamonds. These variations are as numerous as the variations of

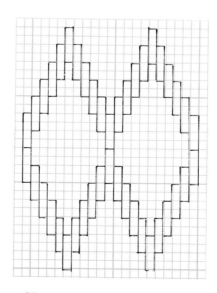

10.

the flame pattern. Sketch 11 shows the fused diamond effect that results from the use of the line in sketch 5. Further changes in design are added by the multitude of possibilities for filling in the diamonds themselves.

A curved row reversed against itself will produce a series of circular medallions. (See sketch 12.) The open spaces between the motifs will create a secondary pattern of small, curved diamond shapes. When color is added, as in the pink and green design on page 79, the design belies the fact that it came from such simple origins.

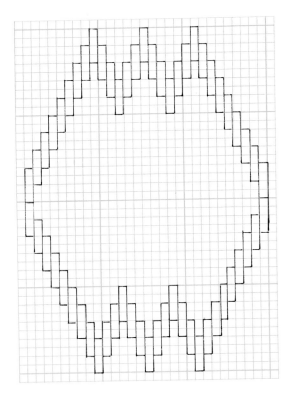

11.

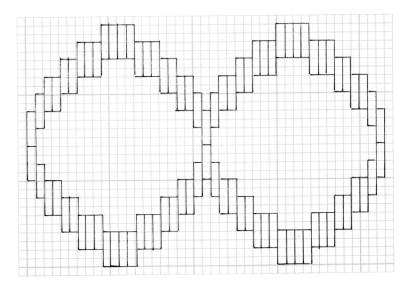

12.

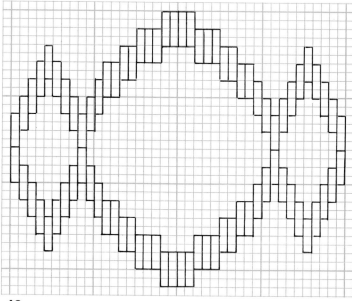

13.

Sketch 13 outlines the interesting motif formed when the basic line incorporates both a curve and a peak. The pink and grey design on page 81 was developed from a line similar to this. The secondary pattern that emerges in the spaces between the motifs was accented by the two-color treatment. A monochromatic arrangement would have given less importance to this "extra" motif, and the design would have appeared less complicated.

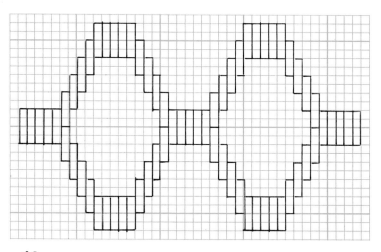

14.

Another possibility for variation of the basic flame pattern is presented in the first row of sketch 14. The top of the flame is flattened through the addition of extra stitches. The development of this pattern by making alterations in step and adding color are shown on page 46 (canvas 12).

If another row of this flattened flame is reversed against the first—both rows share the group of five stitches—the result is a series of hexagonal shapes. (See sketch 14.) This kind of line formed the basis for the design on page 74. Interesting handling of the interior spaces of the hexagons adds to the appeal of the design. Many other arrangements would also be attractive.

Two rows of a curved pattern will form an interesting shell or scale pattern when one is placed under the other so that the center stitch of the widest group is placed directly under the stitch common to the curves in the row above. (See sketch 15.) These shell shapes appear and reappear in Bargello designs for they are very adaptable but at the same time very easy to set up. The rose and green sample on page 88 makes use of the scale line for its basic line.

This breakdown of pattern formations is, of course, very much simplified, but it offers an insight into the principles behind much more complicated design. Beginning with these lines and formations and experimenting with changes within them will result in an understanding of how even the most complicated designs are formed. After that the development of new designs is within easy grasp.

The purpose of the collection of simplified sketches is to help the beginner (1) see how the basic lines can be changed to create new patterns; (2) see how one design builds on another to form still another pattern; and (3) look at a finished sample and see the basic line on which it was built. Bargello is not difficult when one understands the way the designs are constructed. This chapter is the nucleus upon which it is possible to build worlds of new and original design.

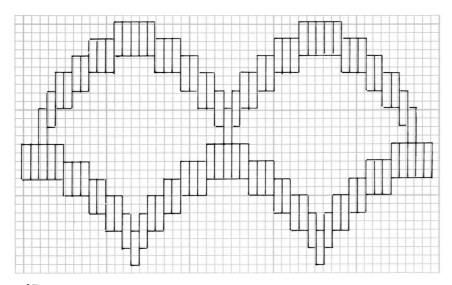

15.

CANVAS 7

5
THE
DESIGNS

This collection of Bargello designs is varied and runs the gamut from the simplest of flame patterns to the complicated Florentine-type embroidery. Some of the designs are completely original, and others are the author's variations of favorite old patterns. The collection can by no means be considered to contain all the Bargello patterns, but it will be a good source of inspiration for many projects.

It is possible to work Bargello designs either from a chart or by actually counting the stitches from a photograph of a finished piece. Very often the stitches are fuzzy when the photograph is enlarged making this process of counting more difficult than it need be. These are very clear photographs, and the design can be counted from them, but as an added convenience a chart has been drawn for each of these designs. A chart does have advantages that may also be helpful to those who are going to count from the photographs. The artist has picked out the most important lines or has isolated the repeat so that it is easy to see. This will make working the design much easier and very often shows at a glance that the basis for the pattern is really very simple.

Work in either manner that you prefer. Notes in the captions list the colors used, suggest other combinations, sometimes indicate ways to enlarge or reduce the size, and give ideas about the best way to a particular design.

CANVASES 7 AND 8: EASY

As we have seen, the flame pattern is the simplest of all the Bargello patterns. Its simplicity, however, has not detracted from its popularity over the centuries. It has always been the most used and best loved. Part of this may be accounted for by its versatility. Variations are almost infinite, and the pattern adapts well to either traditional or contemporary usage.

The little turquoise flame design (canvas 8, opposite) is a regular repetition of a row of peaks ten stitches high worked in a 4–2 step. Four shades of one color were used for a soft monotone effect, but multicolor stripes would be just as attractive. It is also easy to adjust the scale of the flame pattern by changing the number of stitches in a peak.

The larger design, often called a giant flame (see canvas 7, page 38), is of a type often found on colonial chair seats. This one is worked in shades of gold, green, blue, red, and lavender, which surprises many who believe that all the needlepoint surviving from the colonial period was worked in the muted soft shades that we find so often. When it is possible to see the wrong sides of some of the museum pieces, we often find colors as bright as those we love today. Oxidation and fading of dyes has produced the soft colors we know as colonial. This giant flame variation would be as much at home in a tidewater Virginia mansion as it would be in a chrome and steel furnished home of today.

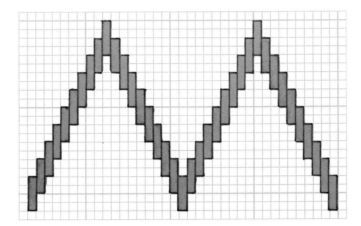

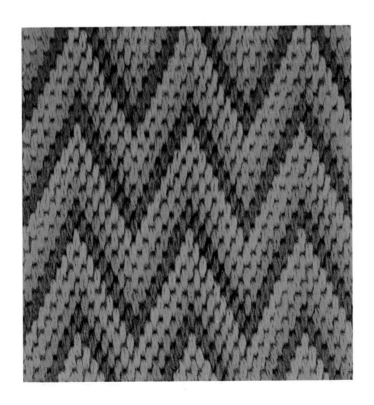

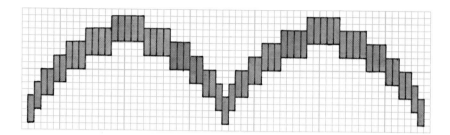

CANVAS 9: EASY

Softest pastel shades of pink, blue, yellow, green, and lavender are used here in a simple repeated scallop. This is another old pattern that can be easily changed in color and scale to adapt to many different situations.

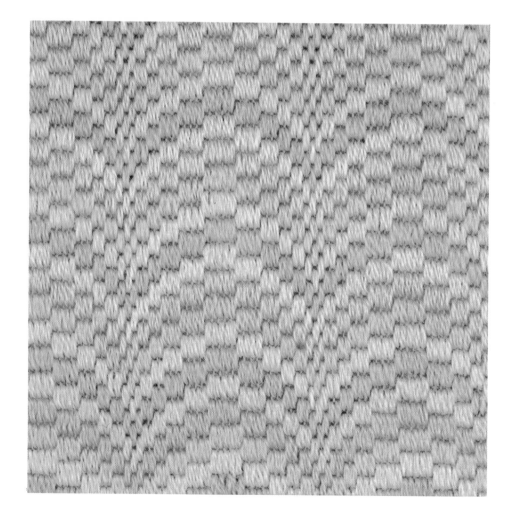

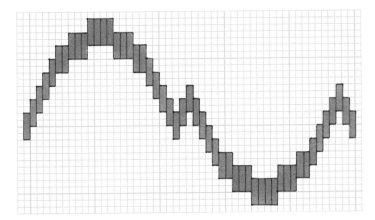

CANVAS 10: EASY

A beautiful old design that does not look as simple as it is, this lovely piece is worked in soft shades of green, old rose, off white, and french blue. Again the step is 4–2, and the design can be easily modified by adding stitches to make the curves larger, the peaks higher, or even by adding additional peaks between the scallops. Four or five shades of one color will work out nicely for a mono-chromatic scheme.

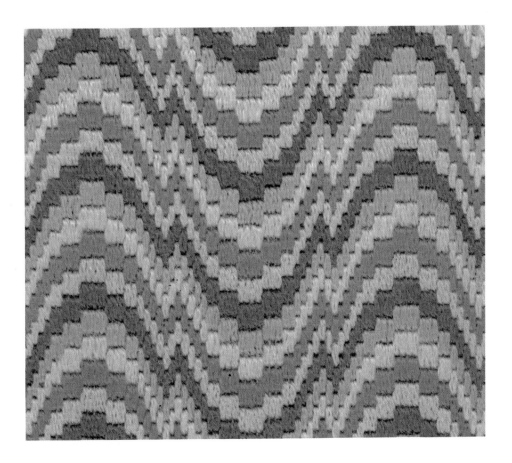

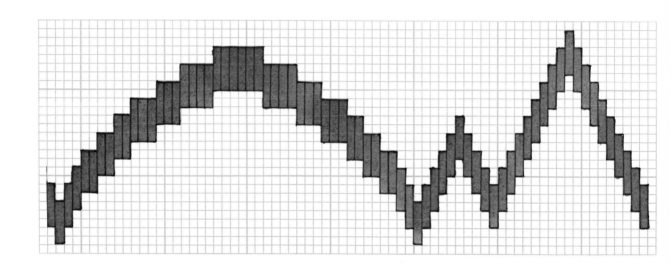

CANVAS 11: EASY

This design is a variation of an old one called "domes and spires." It actually combines the scallops and the flames of canvases 9 and 8. This canvas was worked in five closely shaded golds with two red shades added for a more modern approach. These patterns are very easy to work since the first row establishes the pattern and all subsequent rows merely follow.

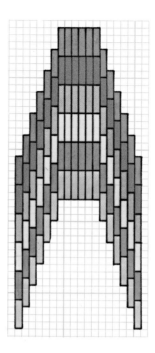

CANVAS 12: EASY

This has great new colors but again a very simple line design. Proof that Bargello designs do not have to be elaborate to be very exciting. Basically this is the flame design but worked in a 4–1 step with six stitches squaring off the top of the peak. This one was fun to work in two bright shades of turquoise, hot pink, orange, and yellow.

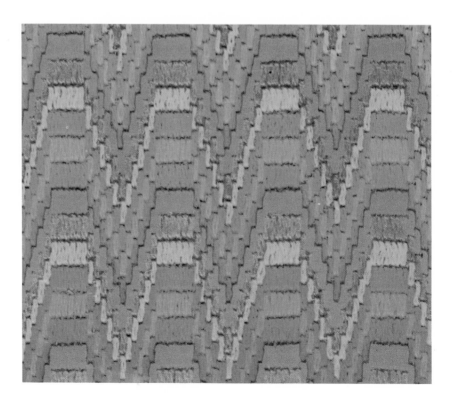

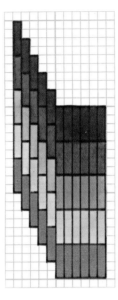

CANVAS 13: EASY

This is a strong diagonal pattern and as shown here is small and neat. It can be made bigger and bolder by adding to the number of steps in the upward slopes and by adding stitches to the wide groups. This is a 4–1 step worked in four golds with a deep reddish orange added.

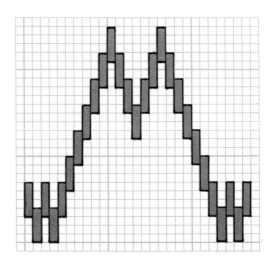

CANVASES 14 AND 15: EASY

This is another flame variation. This one has been worked in a 4–1 step, and the top of the center flame has been widened by the addition of stitches placed saw-toothed fashion. This kind of flame variation was also a favorite in the American colonial period. Here the pattern has been worked in two-color combinations to point up the differences that colors will make in a Bargello design. The softer pink and green version is more in keeping with what we like to think of as colonial, while the brighter one is more contemporary. For the pink one, four shades of old rose were combined with four soft greens. The bolder colored one uses royal blue, bright gold, old gold, bright turquoise, and hot pink.

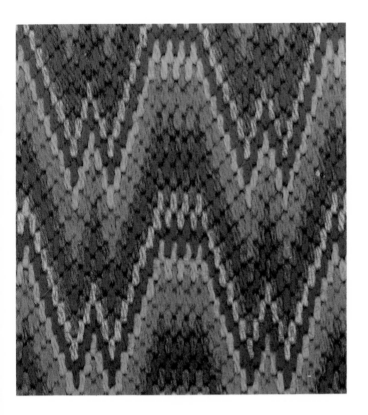

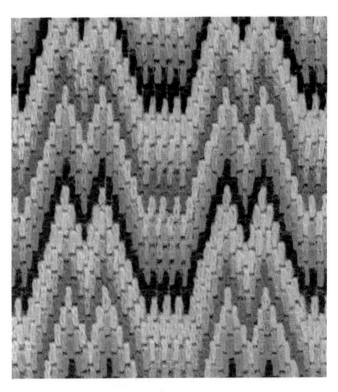

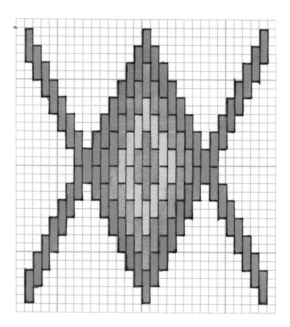

CANVAS 16: EASY

The basic diamond pattern is worked in this version in a 4–2 step using only three shades of old rose. This color scheme creates a very soft look of blended shades. Contrasting colors would make the diamonds stand out much more prominently. Larger diamonds would be the result if more stitches were added to the original line of peaks.

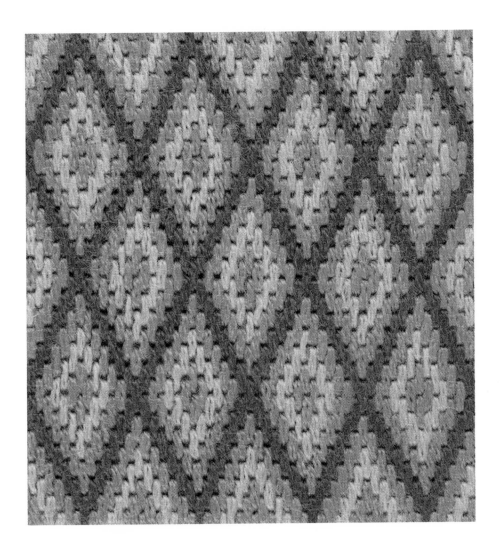

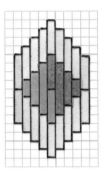

CANVAS 17: EASY

Three soft shades of green were used to fill in the diamonds of this small neat pattern. The 4–1 step makes the diamonds compact, and the method of filling makes the design interesting. This design also presents other possibilities for colors since the use of several different colors would change the overall feeling substantially.

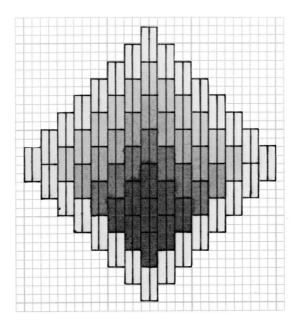

CANVAS 18: EASY

This design looks like shaded boxes, but it is really a basic diamond with the method of filling in creating the three-dimensional effect. Five shades of green were used in a 4–2 step. This is a favorite Bargello design much used because it is easy but looks more complicated. Follow the chart to place the diamonds and work the entire grill that the diamonds form. Then go back and fill in all of one color before beginning to work with the next.

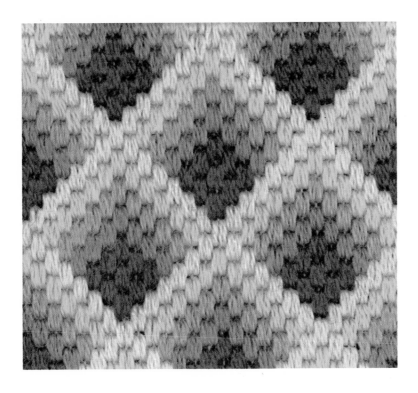

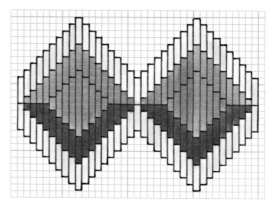

CANVAS 19: EASY

Although the basic design of this piece is simple, it offers many possibilities colorwise. This one has been worked in only three shades of purple, but it would look great in many other colors. The step is 4–1.

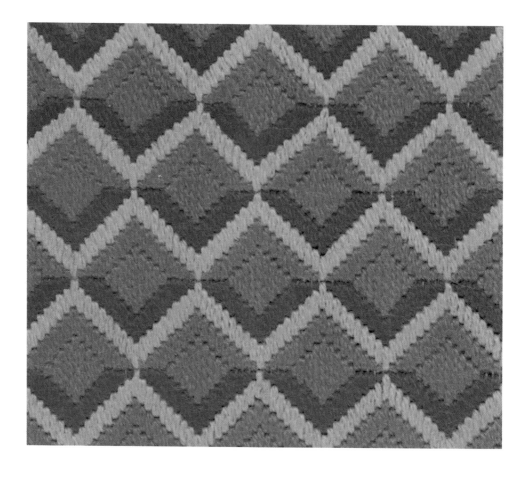

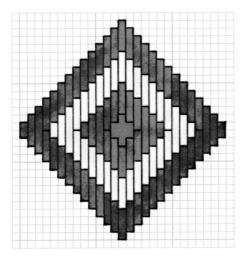

CANVAS 20: EASY

The diamond is used again. These are worked in a 4–1 step and placed on the canvas so that each diamond is a complete unit in itself rather than a part of the adjoining diamond. The colors here are a deep rusty brown, beige, dark green, and burnt orange. The small orange center was a natural for the use of the double cross stitch as a filler instead of the more traditional straight stitch. Little details like this add to the interest of otherwise plain patterns.

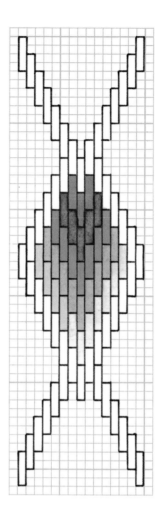

CANVAS 21: EASY

This interesting diamond pattern is five shades of green with three orange stitches accenting the top of the diamond. The way the shapes interlock is emphasized by the use of the contrasting color stitches. This is a 4–2 step throughout. Set the pattern up by working first the pale-green outlines and then work all of each shade before going on to the next.

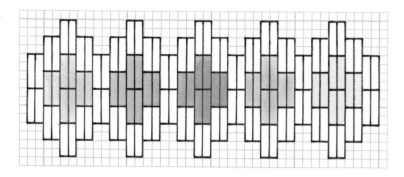

CANVAS 22: EASY

This is an easy little pattern of small diamonds. Work the basic grill of diamonds in the 4–2 step and then fill in with the colors. Bright pastels were used in this sample, but the pattern is equally good with many different color schemes.

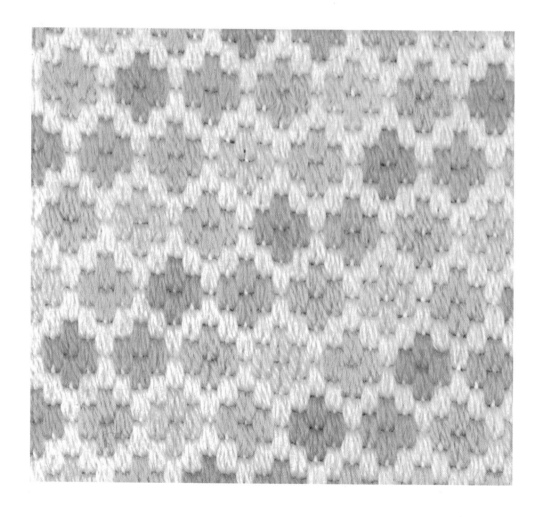

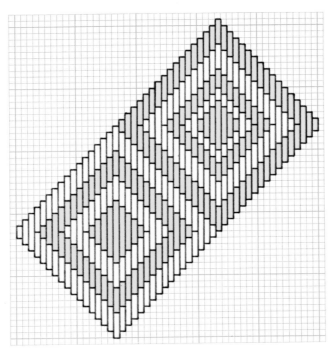

CANVAS 23: EASY

Alternating yellow and white diamonds in this design are slightly larger than in the brown one (canvas 20). Two methods of filling in the spaces are used. The diamond eyelet stitch would also fit the spaces if that look were preferred.

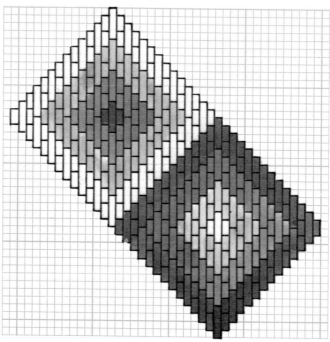

CANVAS 24: AVERAGE

We have talked about the use of stitches other than the Bargello for this embroidery. Here is a Bargello design worked entirely in the Hungarian stitch. The design is again a diamond variation, but it adapts perfectly to the use of the stitch. Three soft shades of french blue and white complete this color scheme.

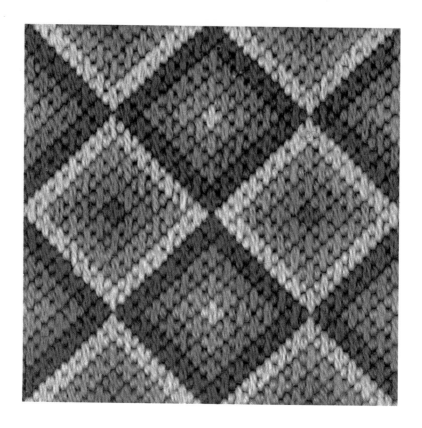

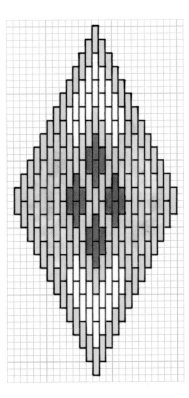

CANVAS 25: AVERAGE

The look of an argyle-knit pattern is achieved here with interlocking diamonds worked in a 4–2 step. Work all of the gold outlines first and then fill in the colors.

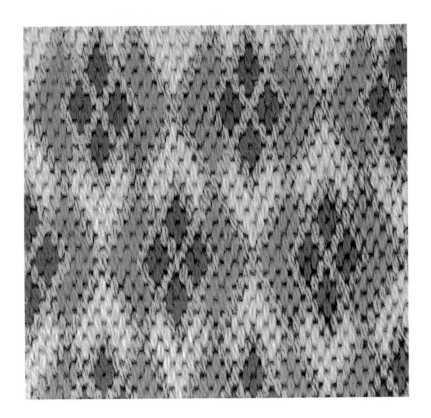

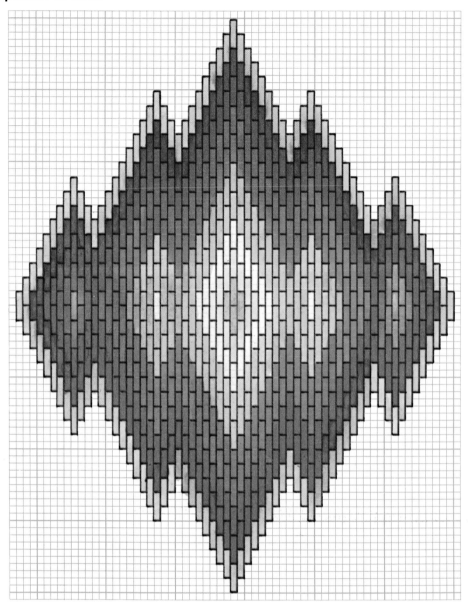

CANVAS 26: AVERAGE

The pale-pink line outlining the diamonds sets the pattern for this design. The method of filling in the center creates the feeling of fused diamonds. Other treatments will change the look completely. A look at the designs on pages 90 and 91 will illustrate this. Both are very similar in their basic line, but the finished effect is very different from this.

For a luster in the center, these diamonds are worked in pale-pink and white embroidery floss. This is a nice accent that draws the eye to the center of the design.

CANVAS 27: AVERAGE

This design is Argyle again, just a little bolder because of the double row of maroon stitches outlining the large diamonds. Work these red rows first, then the royal-blue lines. Fill in the background with brick stitches in gold to complete the design. This is a 4–2 step.

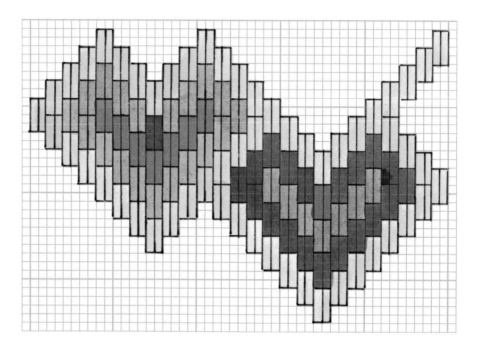

CANVAS 28: AVERAGE

With slight variations in stitches and step this and the following three designs evolved from one basic design. Color treatment also makes a big difference in overall effect. In the blue-green design the chevron pattern is eight steps along its lower edge. The alternating rows are filled in with different colors that bring out the shape of the motif.

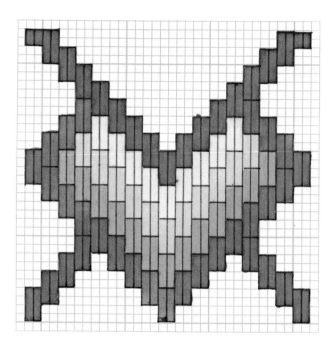

CANVAS 29: AVERAGE

The gold design is worked in only four shades of one color shading downward light to dark. The darkest shade is also the one outlining the chevrons, which makes them seem to interlock rather than to stand out alone as in the first version. Also here the lower edge of the slope is nine steps long enlarging the motif slightly.

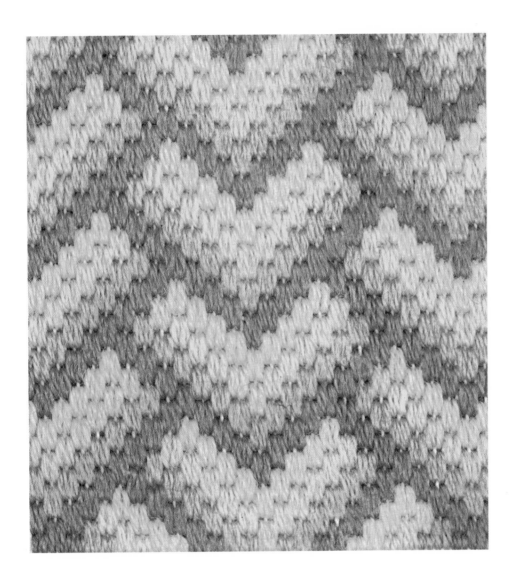

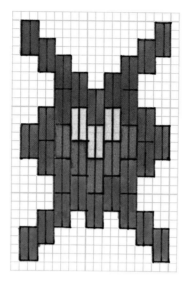

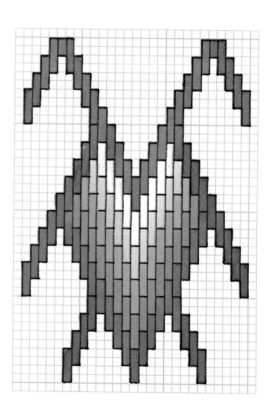

CANVASES 30 AND 31: AVERAGE

The gold, blue, and red version is much smaller—only five steps to the lower edge of the chevron—but interesting in the bright look it gets from its contemporary color scheme. All three were worked in a 4–2 step.

In the all blue design the motif is turned upside down and worked with only one stitch to the step instead of two. The slope of the slanted line is thus much sharper, but the number of steps is the same—ten—as in the gold sample.

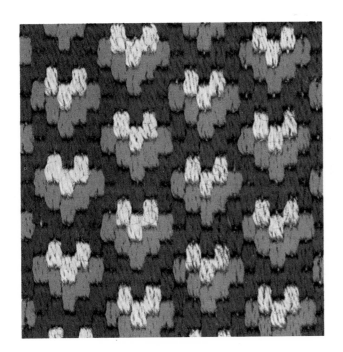

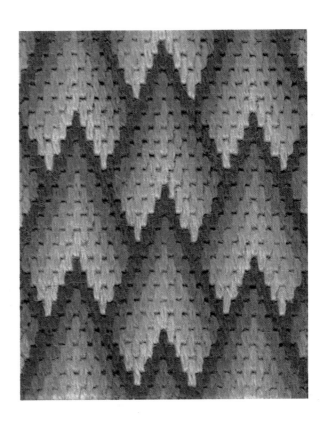

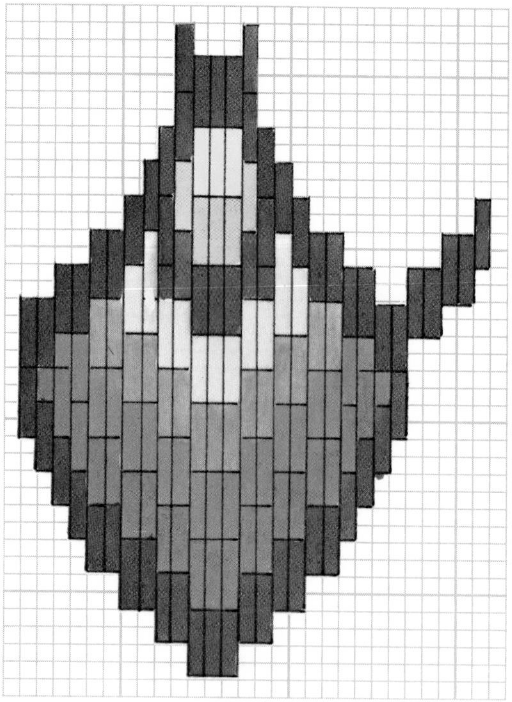

CANVAS 32: AVERAGE

This is another design that is found over and over in historical pieces. This is sometimes called the "fish scale" and sometimes the "eye of the peacock." Usually it is not carried out in such brilliant colors, but it is certainly adaptable to the newer ideas about color as shown here in four brilliant turquoises, red, orange, yellow, and brown. Place the dark brown grill first, and it will be easy to fill in the other colors. Note that there is an adjustment of stitch length along the edge of the motifs to make the curved lines fit. The step here is a 4–1.

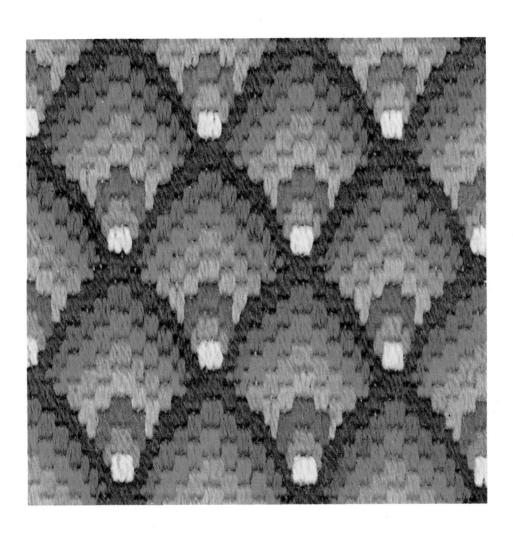

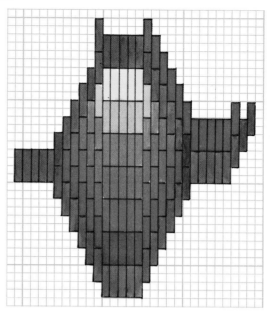

CANVAS 33: AVERAGE

This design is fun to do, for there are so many possibilities for color combinations. It is most effective if worked as shown, shading down from the top, but this does not limit the color combinations. This is a 4–2 step.

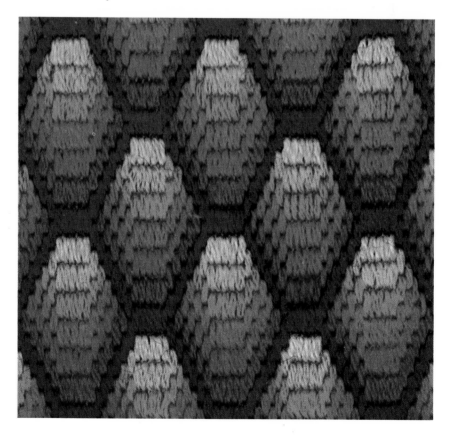

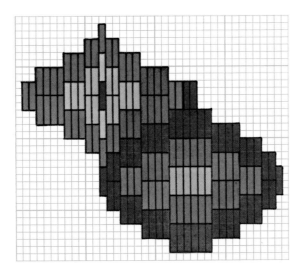

CANVAS 34: AVERAGE

This is emerald green and royal blue in a design of small proportions but much interest. The royal-blue lines should be worked first and the green areas filled in later. Different arrangements of the colors will accent other aspects of the design. This is a very versatile little pattern.

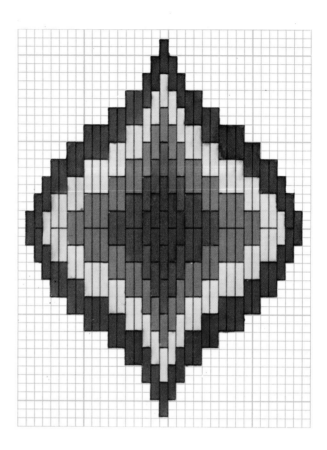

CANVAS 35: AVERAGE

The dark-red continuous line establishes the pattern for the motifs, which are filled in with four shades of red. Worked in a 4–2 step, this type of design is very typical of old Bargello designs. The bright-color treatment makes the design as new as today in this monochromatic sample, but there is no need to stick to a one color scheme. Bright multicolors are great in this kind of design and will really change the look.

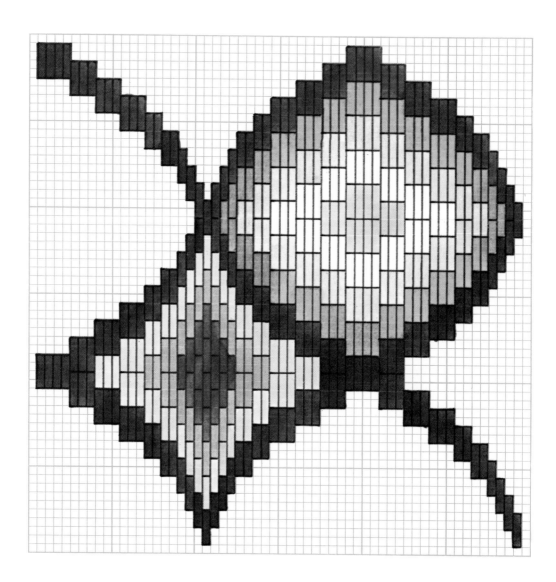

CANVAS 36: AVERAGE

Three greens, three soft pinks, and off white are used here in a pattern composed of fairly large circular motifs. This is a 4–2 step and a very traditional Bargello motif. These soft colors are in keeping with that feeling, but bright colors will make this a very modern design.

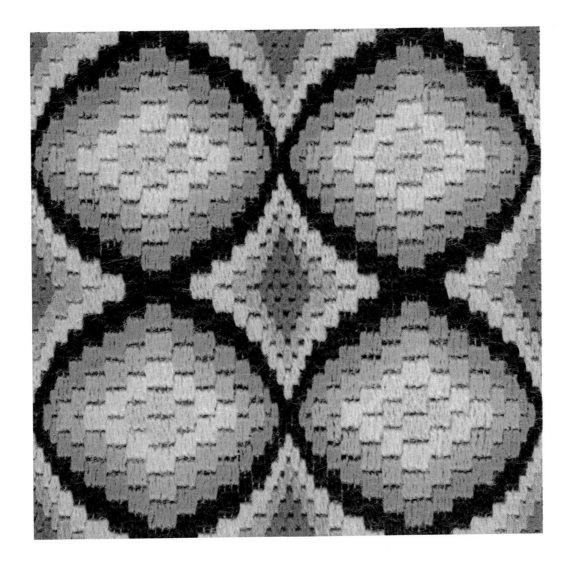

CANVAS 37: AVERAGE

A look at the dark-grey line that outlines the motifs of this design reveals that the pattern is formed by reversing a row of the old "domes and spires" against itself. The spaces thus formed are then filled in to accentuate the lines. Shades of colors are most effective in this type of design, and the ones used here are three greys, white, and four graduations of old rose. The step is 4–2. If the dark-grey lines are placed first, filling in the motifs follows easily.

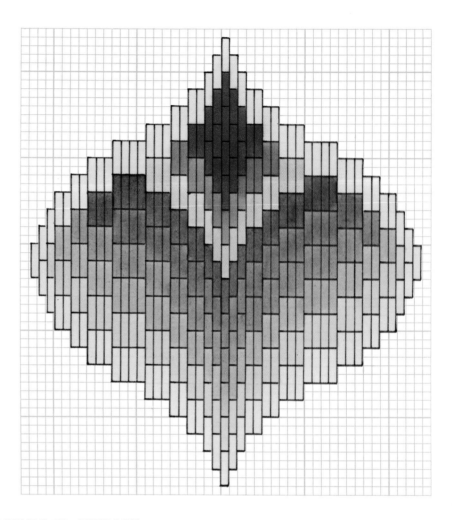

CANVAS 38: AVERAGE

Dark-green heart-shaped motifs alternate with small rose-colored diamonds to make a bold pattern. The very pale-green row will set up the pattern for the motifs, which are then filled in using six closely graded shades of green and three pinks. This 4–2 step design is one of the Bargello patterns that use the optical illusion. A change in the direction of the shading will greatly alter the overall effect.

CANVAS 39: AVERAGE

The blue monochromatic design is a slightly smaller version of the previous pattern with changes in both the coloring and the shading. The effect is to make the whole design softer with less of a definition between motifs.

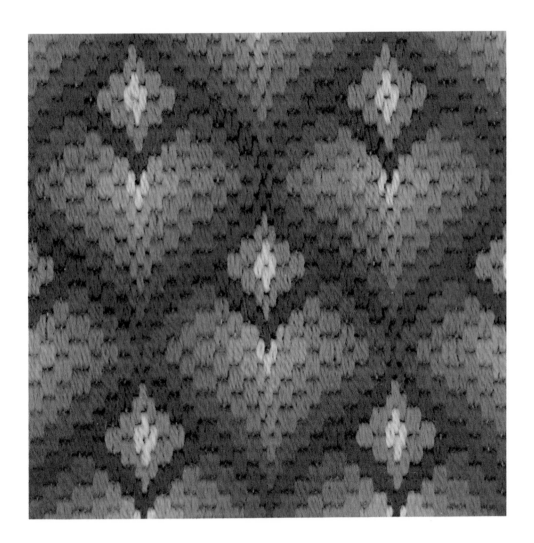

CANVAS 40: AVERAGE

This is a traditional Bargello design updated with colorful modern yarns. The dark-brown outline sets the pattern, which is not nearly as involved as it appears at first glance. The many colors set the motifs out in bright contrast to their neighbors and make them seem much more important than they would have if the design had been worked in a one-color scheme. The colors used for this sample were four shades of turquoise, off white, and four each of brown, burnished gold, and red.

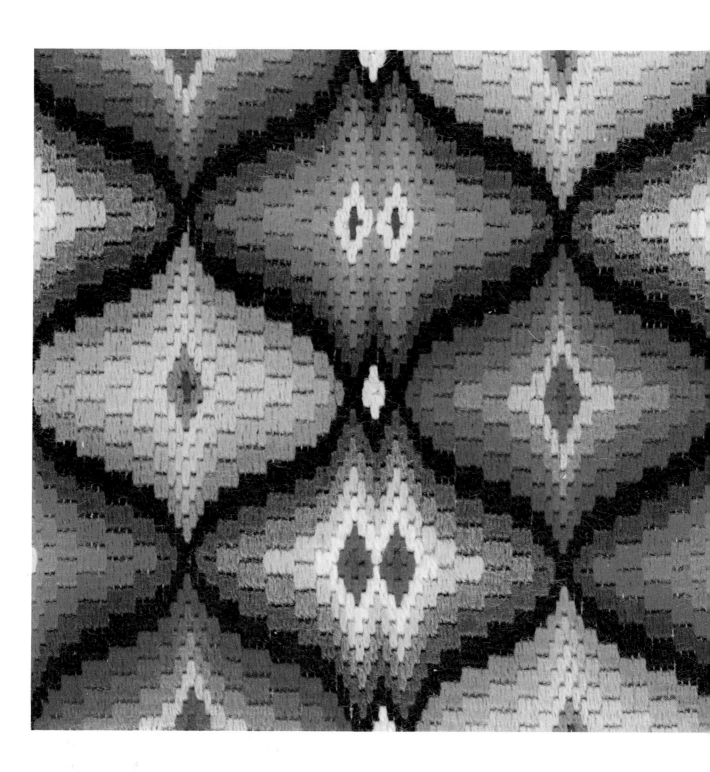

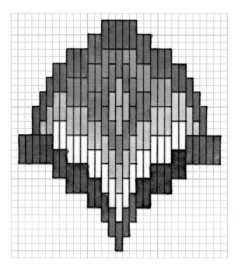

CANVAS 41: AVERAGE

A small shell-shaped motif here is softly shaded, and a green diamond is added in the center to relieve the monotony of such a simple repeat. The deep-rose row is a continuous line establishing the pattern in a 4–2 step. Four delicate rose shades are used with two complimenting greens.

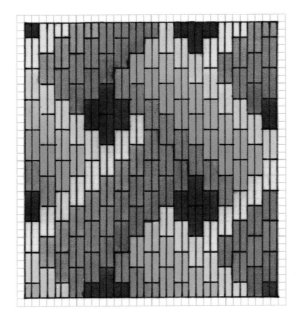

CANVAS 42: AVERAGE

For obvious reasons this design is known as the basket weave. Actually a pattern easy to set up, it is composed of four rows of stitches in steps placed so that the groups of rows seem to interlock. The four brown stitches fill in the spaces left and add depth. The gay combination of colors in the sample are four oranges and four shades of aqua. The step is 4–2.

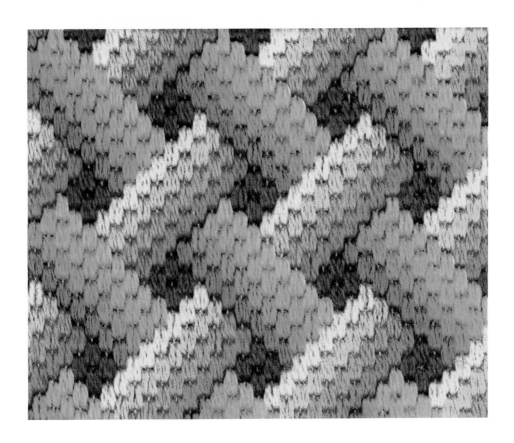

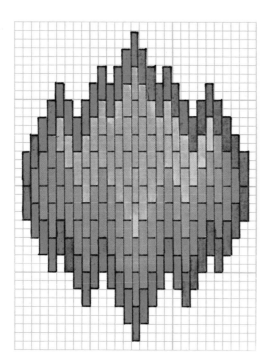

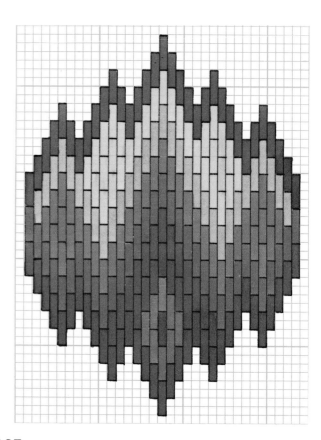

CANVASES 43 AND 44: AVERAGE

One of the fascinating things about Bargello is that once the basic line establishing a pattern has been placed there are so many ways of filling in the spaces that many different effects are possible. The line in these two samples is the same except for minor variations, but the shading makes them appear unlike. Other treatments produce different effects making this a very versatile pattern.

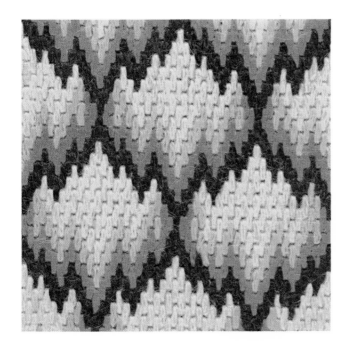

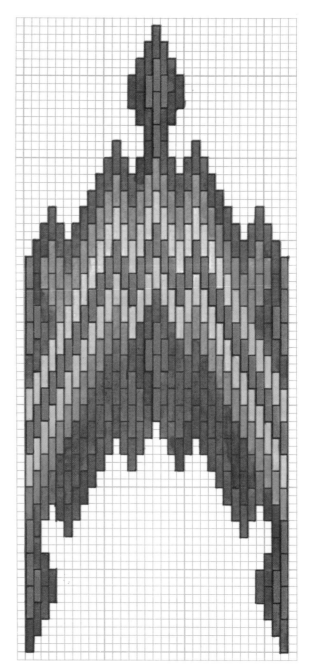

CANVAS 45: AVERAGE

This is an interesting design in a 4–2 step. Four shades of green are enlivened with a row of red-orange. It is best to work the dark-green row first and then follow the chart working downward one row at a time until the next dark-green row is reached. Some of the rows are continuous and others are not. Following the chart for the first repeat will avoid confusion.

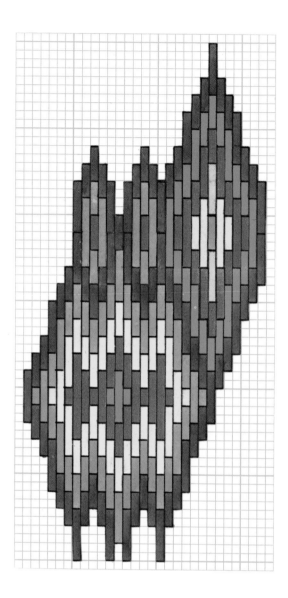

CANVAS 46: AVERAGE

This design looks at first as if it should be classified as advanced. The many colors perhaps make it look more complicated than it really is. The royal-blue line establishes the pattern line, and the other colors follow with some minor changes in the length of stitches inside the motifs. The chart shows these adjustments as well as the color placement. Combined with the royal blue are a pink-red, yellow, deep aqua, and bright green. Except for the places where adjustments are made, the step is a 4–2. This one is also fun to experiment with by changing the colors to get different looks.

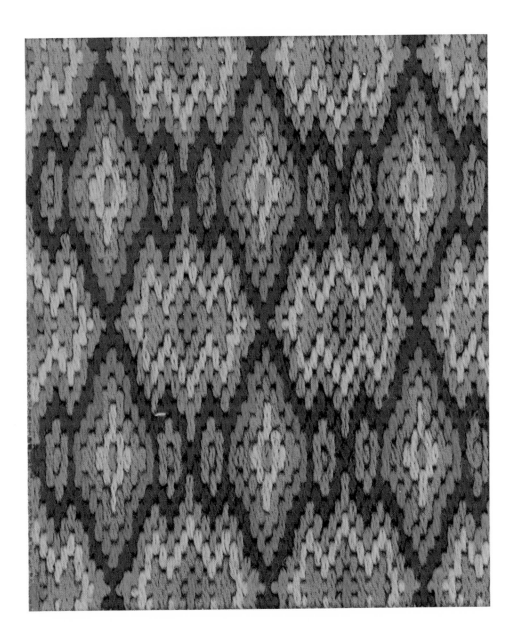

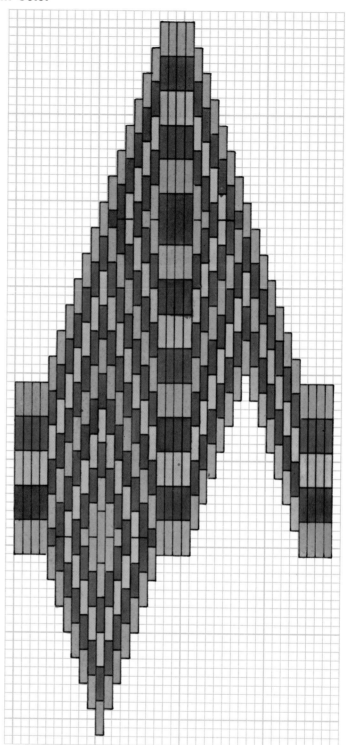

CANVAS 47: AVERAGE

The bright colors and the way the design took shape made this pattern fun to work. This is a 4–1 step in royal blue, red, orange, kelley green. Place the two central green rows that form the diamond first, then follow the rows outward for the balance of the pattern.

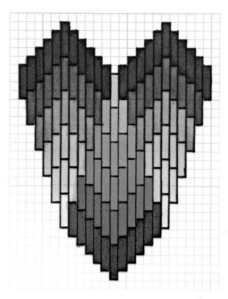

CANVAS 48: AVERAGE

Alternating shapes of blue and gold combine to make a simple but attractive design. Six shades of each color were used, but fewer shades could also be used if two or more shades were repeated. This is a 4–1 step.

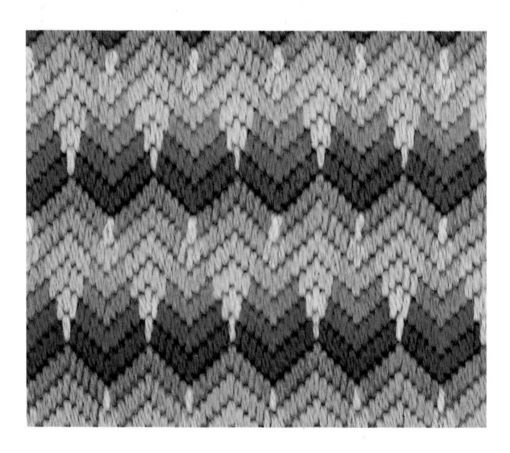

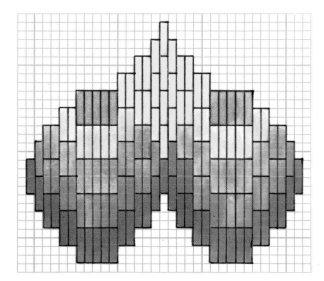

CANVAS 49: AVERAGE

Four shades of blue, one yellow, and one orange combine in an uncomplicated design of small proportions. Work a whole row of motifs beginning with the dark-blue line before going on to the next row. Fill in the yellow diamonds last. This is a 4–2 step.

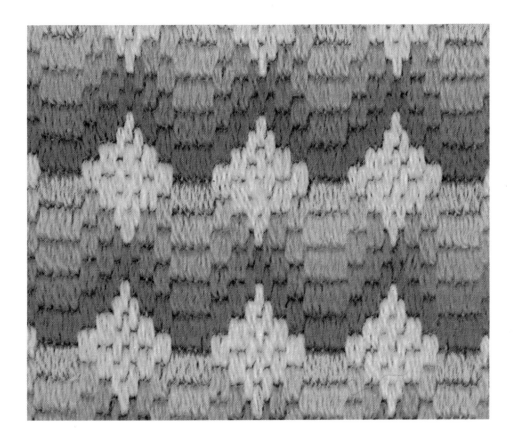

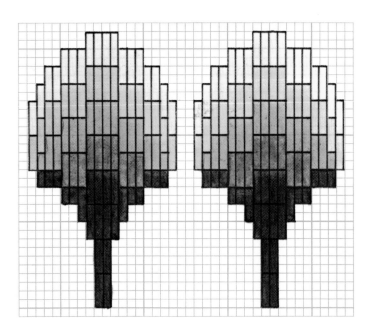

CANVAS 50: AVERAGE

This design consists of row upon row of little trees, which were worked in four shades of a khaki green. Autumn colors or spring greens would be interesting changes, or you could go all the way with fantasy and use bright pastels. Five shades of green were used in this 4–2 step.

CANVAS 51: AVERAGE

A pattern-on-pattern effect is achieved here by placing the large white diamonds over the simple flame pattern. The flame pattern continues its regular repeat under the diamonds. Using a 4–2 step place the double rows of white that form the large diamonds. Then work in the flame background following the chart. Four shades of french blue were combined with the white for a subdued effect.

multiple of 33 +1

+ 44 high

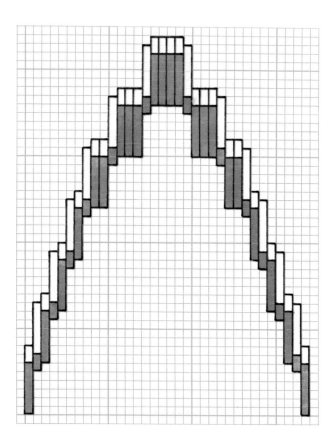

CANVAS 52: AVERAGE

This is a wonderful pattern—fast to work and adaptable to so many color combinations. The step is 6–1, which is the reason it is so fast to work. The colors here are soft shades of french blue, off white, olive green, and two rose shades.

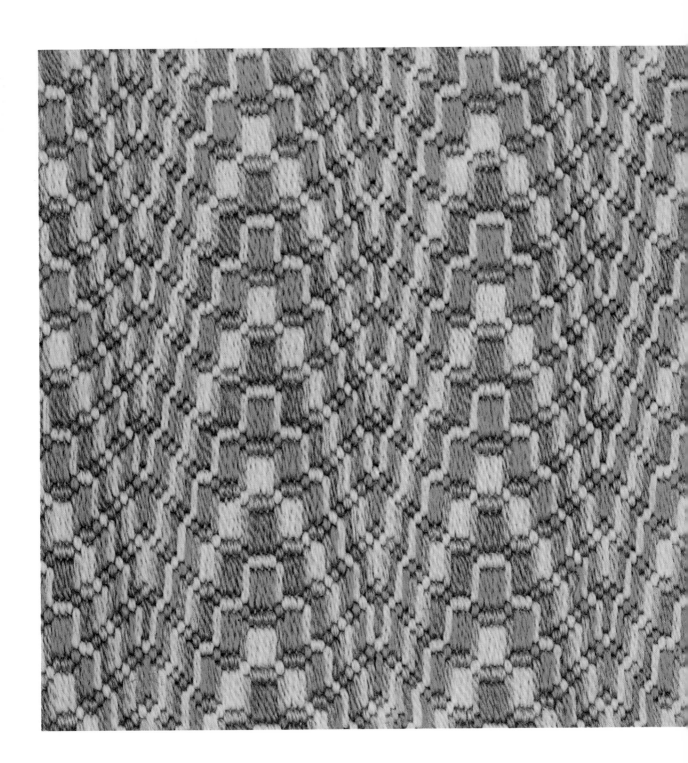

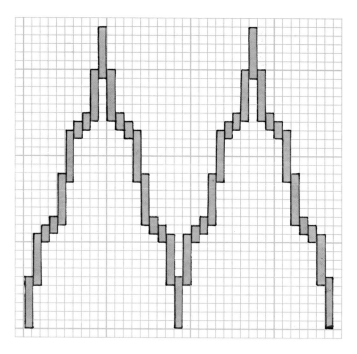

CANVAS 53: ADVANCED

Patterns such as this one that combine stitches of two lengths are often called Florentine embroidery. The use of the dual-stitch length makes working a little more complicated, but the designs are singularly attractive and have as a bonus the secondary pattern created by the short stitches. If worked all in one color, the second pattern becomes more visible in a brocaded effect. (See red background of border design on page 115.)

This version uses the Florentine stitching in a pattern of regular peaks worked in two shades of mauve, one lavender, and white. This is a 6–1 step. To avoid confusion the chart shows only the lavender row. It is easy to keep track of the change in stitch length if you remember that two short stitches are always placed under two long stitches. This is the key to not getting lost in these patterns.

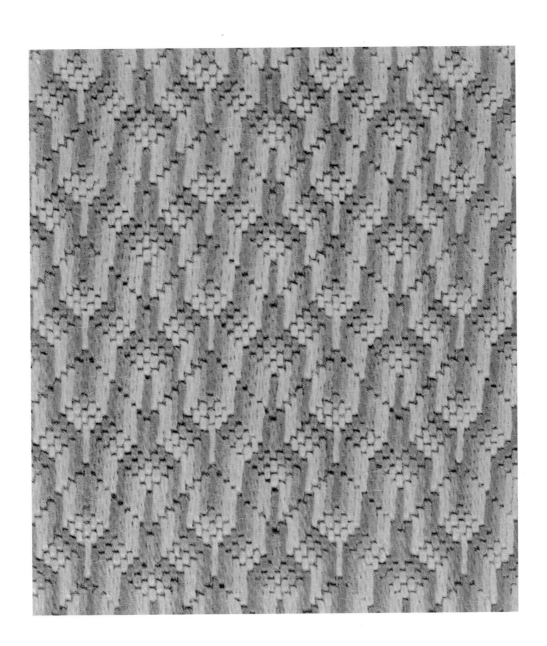

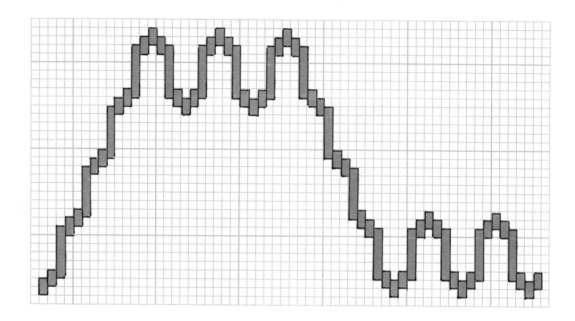

CANVAS 54: ADVANCED

The Florentine stitches are used again in a 6–1 step with bright colors and an interesting line. Three aquas, one yellow, and two oranges are combined. Work the darkest row all the way across the canvas and follow with the subsequent colors. Check to make sure that you are always keeping the pattern of two short stitches under two long ones or the rows will not work out right.

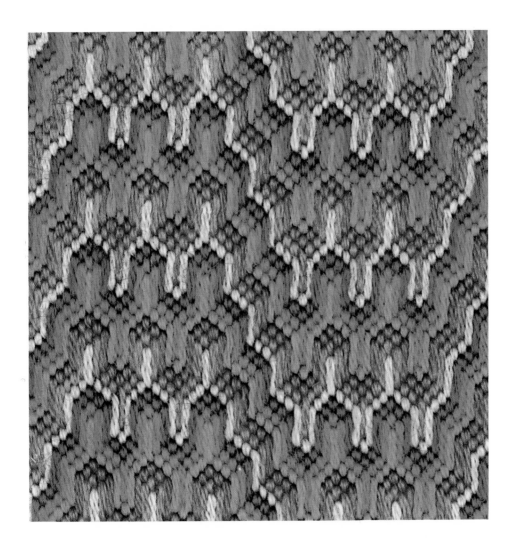

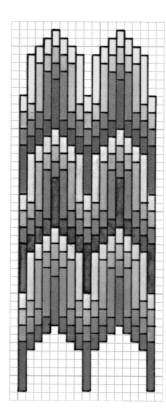

CANVAS 55: ADVANCED

Rows of bright color update a favorite old wishbone pattern that is worked Florentine fashion with stitches in two lengths. This is a 6–1 step. When worked as here with four shades of each color the pattern repetition will work out so that the wishbone row is always the darkest shade. This pattern alternates three short stitches with three long ones.

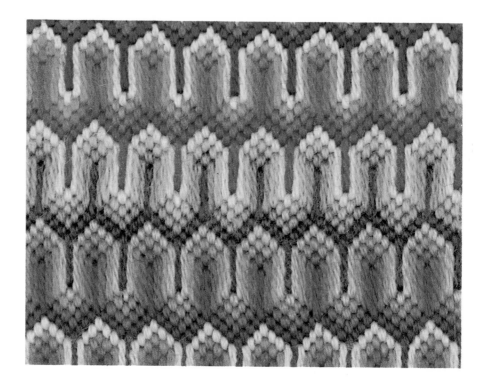

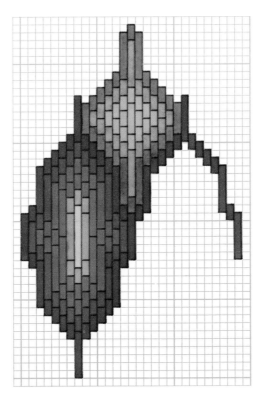

CANVAS 56: ADVANCED

Stitches worked over both six and two threads contribute to the intricacy of this design. The larger medallions are worked in six shades working from dark red through the oranges to pale yellow. Smaller motifs are in four contrasting shades of green. Work in a 6–1 step beginning with the darkest red rows that outline the motifs.

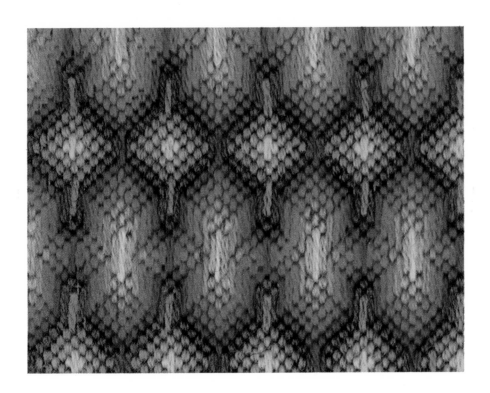

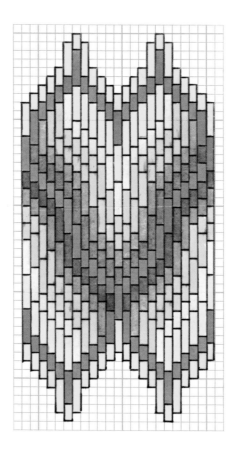

CANVAS 57: ADVANCED

Heart-shaped motifs fit together to form a border worked again in the Florentine stitches. The plain oriental-blue background continues the long and short stitch pattern for a brocaded effect. Pale aqua outlines the motifs and sets up the pattern. Motifs are filled in with three shades of pale-gold wool and a cream-colored cotton six-strand embroidery floss used double (twelve strands to cover the number 13 canvas). The entire border has been outlined with six-strand silk floss in a bright metallic gold. The stitches are worked over four and two threads in a 4–1 step.

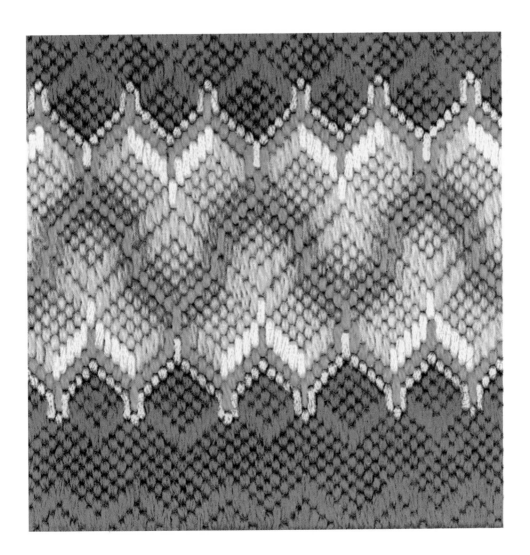

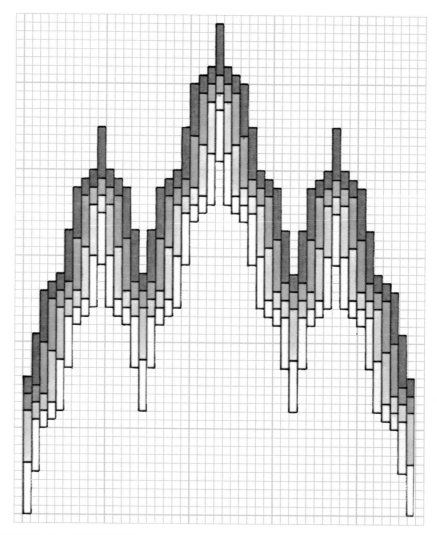

CANVAS 58: ADVANCED

As shown, this design can be used as a border or repeated for a solid pattern. Both ways it is very attractive. The stitches are worked over six and two threads in a 6–1 step. Reading down the row, two long stitches are always followed by two short ones. The textured background is the secondary pattern that is the result of the Florentine stitching—a very attractive bonus. Black, three shades of grey, and white were used against a red background.

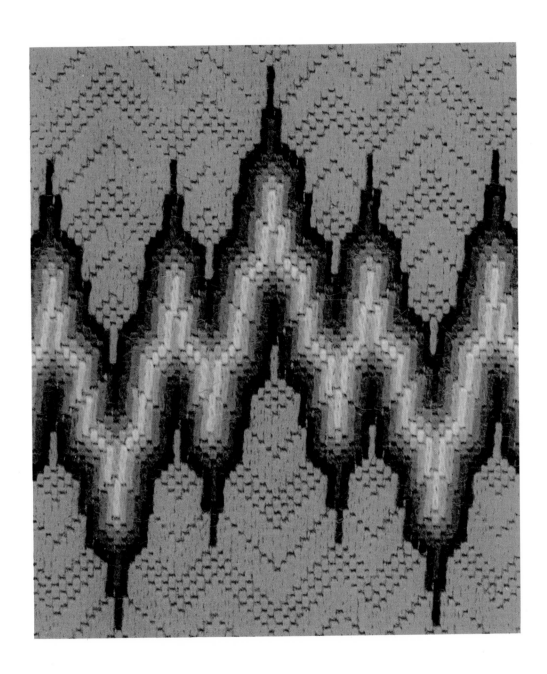

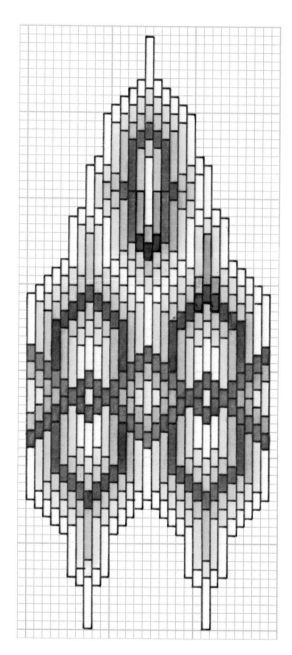

CANVAS 59: ADVANCED

The white row is the most important row in this design since it outlines the motifs. Following the chart, work this row first and then fill in medallions. The step is 6–1. Three shades of green and white were used. The row of diamonds across the center is in rust, burnt orange, and cream. This is another design classified as Florentine embroidery, since it is worked using stitches of two lengths.

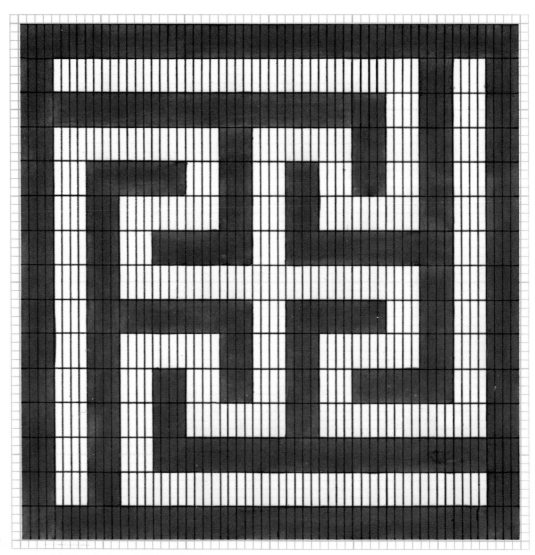

CANVAS 60: ADVANCED

Not really a Bargello pattern, but using the upright Gobelin stitch to create a geometric design, this purple and white square would make a handsome border or center of a larger piece. It illustrates the adaptability of the Gobelin stitch in designing ideas that are not typically Bargello.

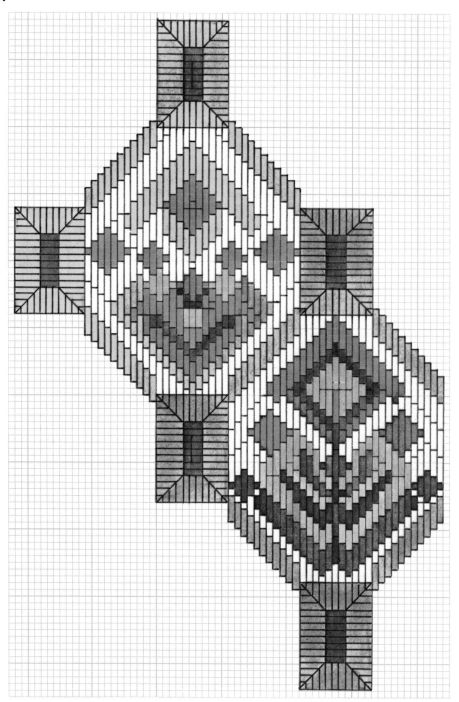

CANVAS 61: VERY ADVANCED

This design is quite intricate and must be carefully counted from the chart, but it will be worth the effort because it is a very original looking pattern. The colors are soft, and the combination is unusual. Stitch length varies over two, four, and six threads to fit the needs of the pattern. The colors are rusty brown, light rust, pink, and cream.

6
MITERED BARGELLO

One of the most exciting and challenging aspects of the new Bargello is the mitered design. To claim that the technique is entirely new would be false because dating from the early eighteenth century there are rugs in museums that show remarkable use of the mitered Bargello for borders. Until lately, however, there has been little attention paid to the possibility of developing these mitered borders into complete designs. Handled in this manner, the mitered or four-way Bargello is definitely new. When the canvas is divided into four triangles and the design worked out from the center in four directions, the simplest of Bargello lines become intriguing patterns. Many of these resemble a kaleidoscope and become very intricate. The manner in which new patterns develop as the lines meet at the corners adds to the fascination of the interplay of color, making the development of these designs very exciting. It is a process full of surprises.

The mitered designs do take more skill and thought than the average Bargello, but once the basics of Bargello are mastered these patterns are within the scope of the thoughtful needleworker. For a first experiment it would be a good idea to begin with one of the designs that develop from a continuous-line pattern and then work into the more complicated patterns involving detached motifs. One of the most interesting things about these patterns is that the simplest of beginning patterns looks wonderfully complicated when it has been translated into a mitered design. There is no hint whatsoever that this easy design was chosen as an uncomplicated beginner's project.

Several mitered designs are photographed and completely charted as an aid in starting this type of work. Although it will be generally true that a person interested in these will probably be advanced enough not to feel the need for a chart, the charts do have the advantage of being very explicit in showing the details of changing the stitch length necessary to mitering the corners. Corners are a bit of a problem in the beginning, but as one works, the needed changes become readily apparent.

To make a neat diagonal line where the sections meet—the miter —the length of some of the stitches must be altered. The accompanying drawing shows the adjustments that make a neat line. The

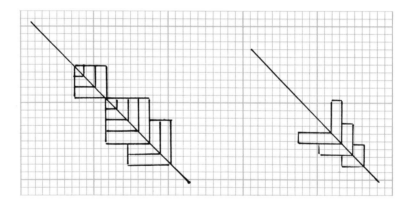

stitches are shortened so that they fit exactly along the diagonal line. In the instance where a stitch worked over four threads to match its mates would have left a space only one thread long for the stitch of the next row, this stitch was instead lengthened to five. Stitches worked over only a single thread do not lie as neatly as they could and should be avoided if possible. However, there will arise situations where there is no solution except this very short stitch. Each possibility will have to be examined when the miter is reached, and the method that looks best in each case decided then.

This same chart shows the method of handling the miter when a group of stitches is involved. The bottom edge of the stitches is kept even, only the tops of the stitches affected are adjusted. This maintains the patterns but at the same time allows for the neat mitering line.

To set up a mitered design, first divide the canvas into four triangles by drawing two diagonal lines that intersect in the center mesh of the canvas. Use either a waterproof marker or a length of yarn, as was used in the illustration. Be very careful when placing this line to draw it accurately through the corners of the mesh. This line indicates where the stitching direction will change. All of the adjustments in the length of stitches will also occur on these lines.

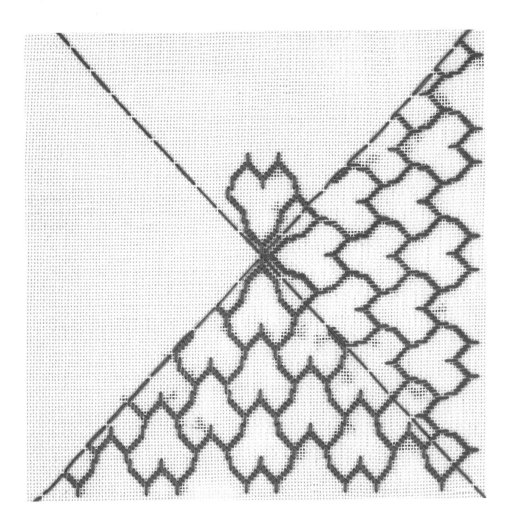

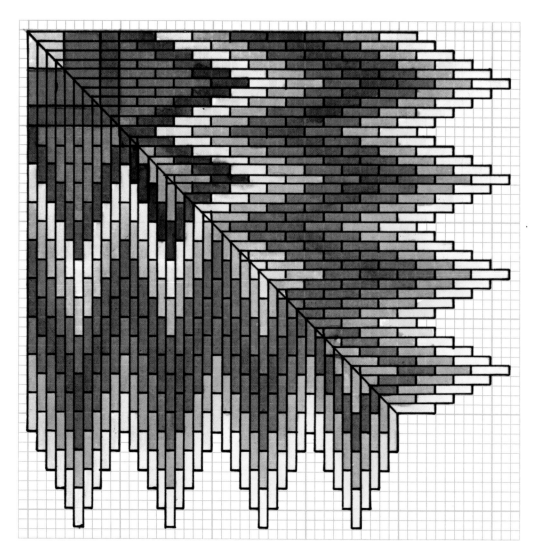

An easy flame-stitch row forms the basic pattern for the mono-chromatic blue design shown here. With this type of continuous-row design it is best to begin working with a row placed about mid-way down into the first segment. In this particular one it was the darkest blue that was used to establish the pattern.

Center the flame pattern by beginning to work in the middle of the row and working out to the mitering line. End the yarn, and go back again to the center and work out to the miter at the other side of the segment. By following the pattern thus established it will now be possible to work in rows completely around the square. Work in toward the center completing that part of the design before finishing the outside edges.

This design was worked in four shades of one of the blue families. The feeling of the whole pattern would have been changed if the color scheme had involved more colors or families of colors. The

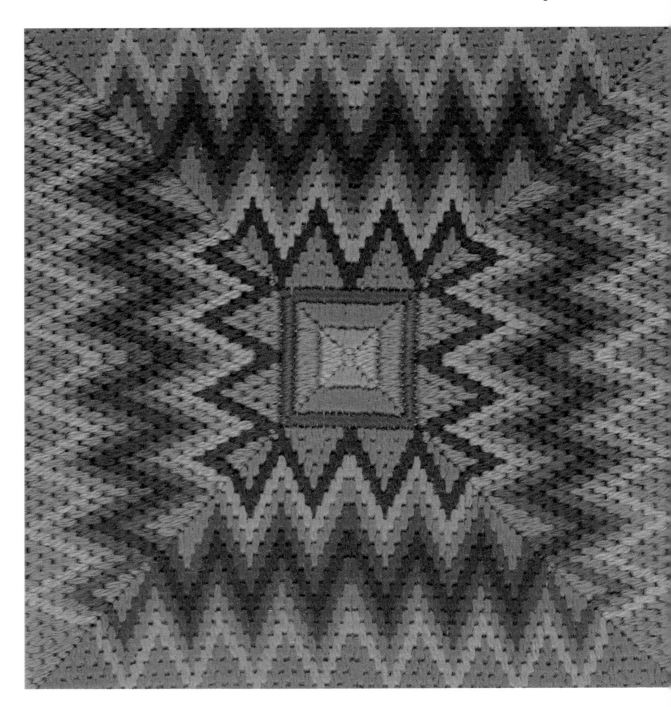

size of this type of design is easily adjusted by just adding rows to
the outside edges.

The edges of this design were squared off by filling in the spaces
between the points with the brick stitch in one of the light-blue
shades. This area could just as easily have been completed with the
tent stitch. This would have had the effect of making the design itself
stand out more prominently from its background.

A close look at the green monochromatic design shown here reveals that this delicate pattern is derived from the old favorite "domes and spires" pattern. The curves and peaks give surprising new interest where they intersect along the miter. This is another continuous-line pattern that is best established by a center row that is then joined and worked around and around the canvas. The first row in this piece was the dark olive-green. The other three shades of green follow through to the palest yellow-green. The tent stitch was used for the background, affording a pleasant contrast in stitch texture.

The size of this design can be altered by adding or subtracting rows at the outer edges. This feature makes these designs adaptable to a variety of sizes.

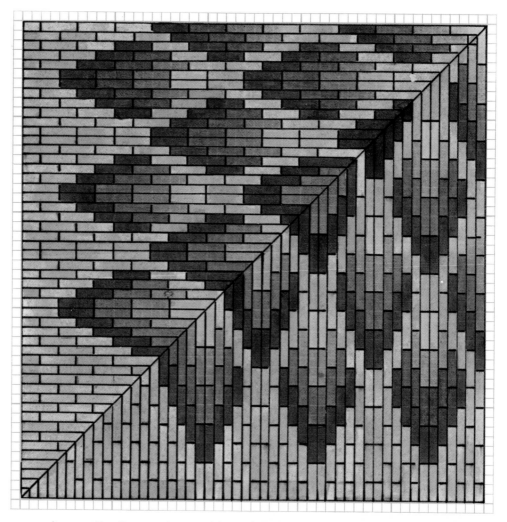

A small diamond provides the basis for this dainty design. Four shades of purple are outlined in pink. The pattern was established by first placing the four centered diamond motifs. Then the entire pink framework was worked over the canvas to set up the pattern. This gets all the counting out of the way in the beginning and leaves the easy part to finish. Although the pattern motif is different, the photograph on page 125 shows the method of setting up a pattern in this manner. It is then very easy to go along and fill in the diamonds one shade at a time to complete the piece.

Alterations in this kind of design are easy to make. The size of the diamond can be increased or reduced. The method of filling in the diamonds can be changed—even so slight a change as a shift in the direction of the shading will produce a great deal of difference in the overall design. To increase the size of this piece it is necessary only to continue to add rows of motifs. With the addition of new rows, each corner will develop a new pattern that will contribute to the design interest.

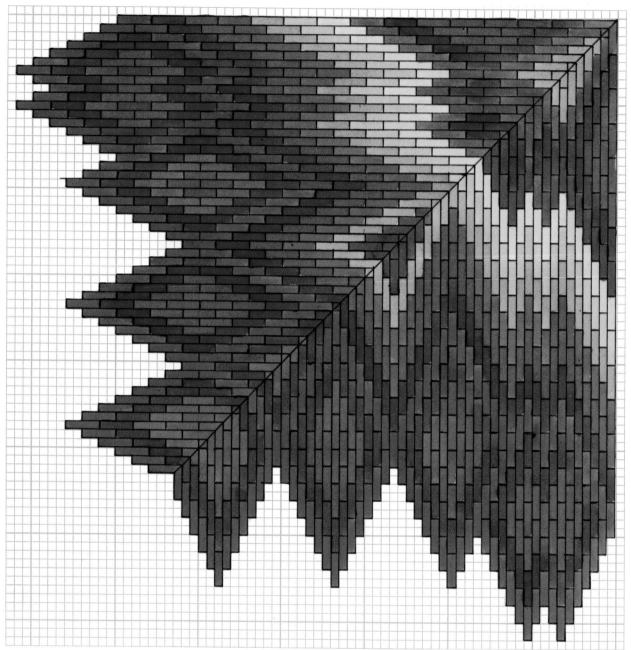

The beginning for the lively design shown here was a large diamond with two smaller fused diamonds on each side. When these were placed, the blue line became continuous and could then be followed around and around the canvas. As the colors shaded out from pale yellow through the oranges to the reds, the pattern grew and the next blue line merely followed it. The diamonds around the edge were a natural outgrowth of the blue line. If a larger piece had been needed it would have been fun to continue to add diamonds in the same manner.

This design has been worked in one shade of pale yellow, three of orange, two reds, and royal blue. Surprising differences will come about with changes in color arrangement.

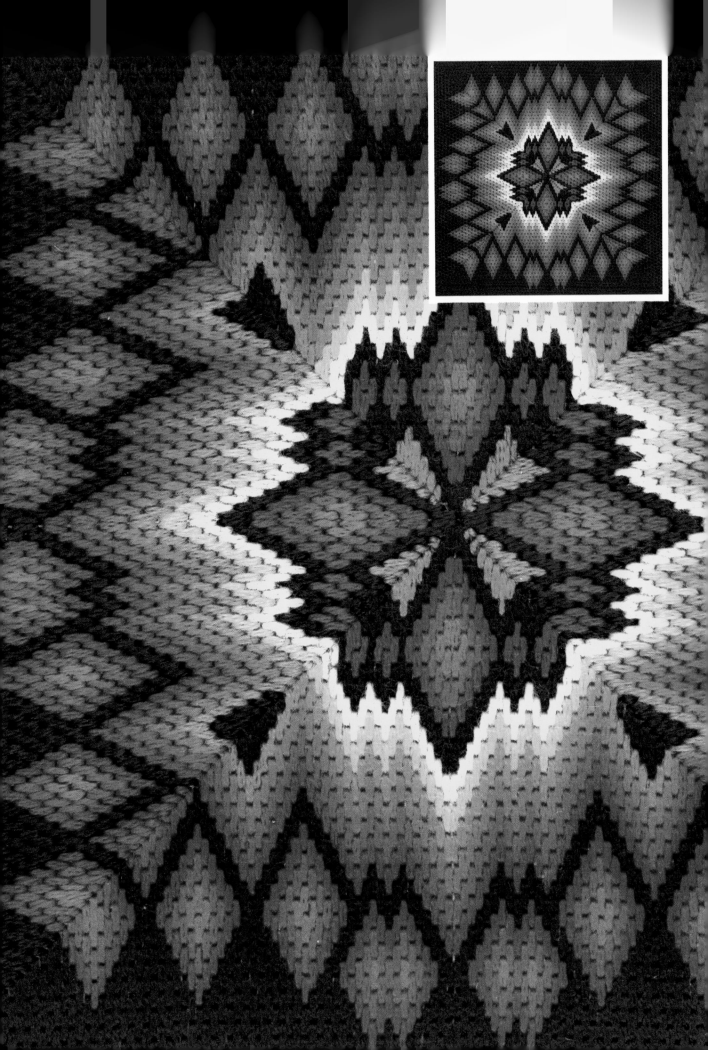

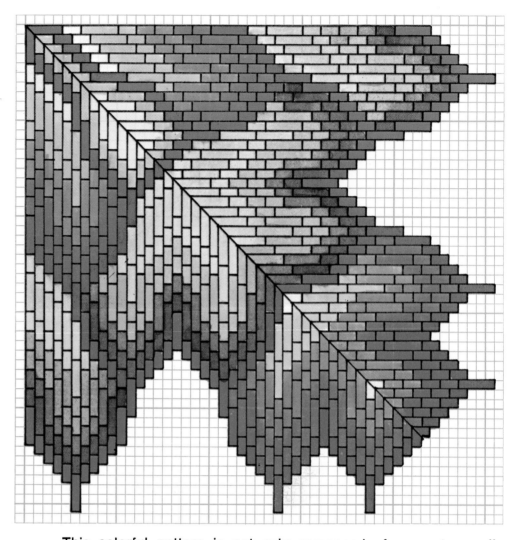

This colorful pattern is not only composed of separate small motifs but also uses the Florentine embroidery technique of making stitches of two different lengths. This is very interesting to work out. The center motifs were placed first. Then the dark-turquoise outlines of the motifs were plotted over the entire canvas. This is the design shown on page 125. This gets all the counting out of the way and establishes that the pattern is well adapted to mitering. The motifs are then filled in by using four shades of turquoise and five shades of gold. The lightest of the turquoise family is six-strand-cotton embroidery floss. The next-to-the-darkest gold is pure-silk embroidery thread—also six strand. The sheen of these two materials contrasts nicely with the soft wools of the other colors.

Changing the length of the longer stitches from four to six would slightly alter this design as would changes in coloring. A monochromatic scheme would work out very nicely, but there is no reason why a number of colors could not be introduced if needed. Additional rows of motifs will increase the size, and widening the plain outside borders would add another interest when the brocaded effect of the two lengths becomes more prominent.

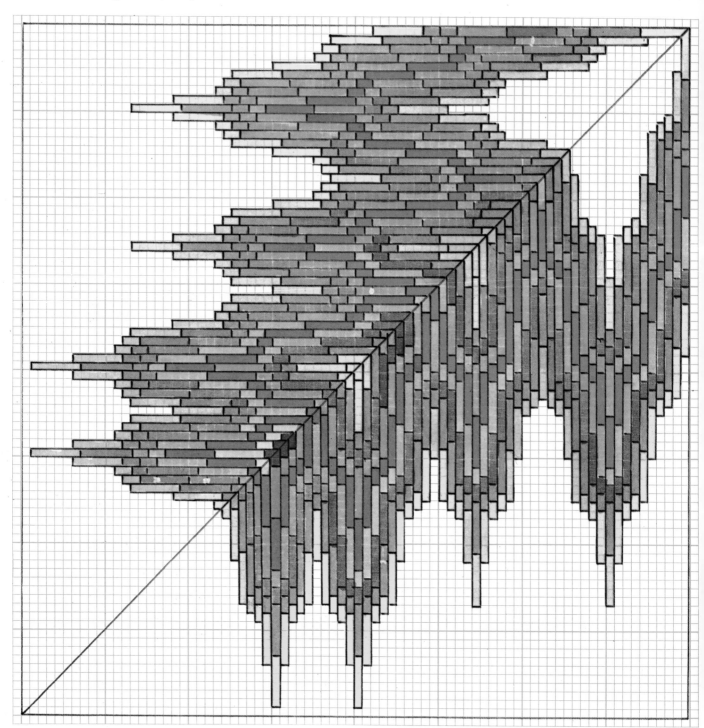

The principle for the basic line of the pattern shown here was taken from the border shown in black and grey on page 115. This time the border was worked in one shade of yellow, one orange, one pink-red, and two turquoise. The colors are used from the palest

yellow through the orange and red to the deepest aqua, which is the center row. The shades then continue in reverse order to the outside edge. This is one of the Florentine-type embroidery patterns in which stitches are of two lengths and the rows are not exact repeats, and so the design was first plotted on graph paper so that it would work out that the yellow rows at the outside edges would be alike. Plotting the design on paper also made working out the portion where the miter interrupts the line easier. It is much simpler to erase a pencil mark than to rip out a whole series of stitches. This is where graph paper can save a lot of time.

This design with its bright colors and complicated line needed an unobtrusive background, and so it was placed against the tent stitch worked in the palest of the turquoise shades. It would have been faster to finish the edges in Florentine stitches of the same shade. The brocaded effect thus produced would have also been a good background for the design.

Not all designs will adapt well to the mitering technique, but so many can be modified that the possibilities seem unlimited. A trial "run" on graph paper will usually point out any problems that a particular design may present. It is not necessary to plan an entire design on graph paper. Just plan the center motifs to establish the pattern and then begin working on the canvas, letting the design grow as you work outward. It is really much more fun to figure out the design as you go. The surprising little things that happen as you work make it most interesting. The corners are perhaps the best part. Even after you have worked several mitered designs you will find that the corners are full of surprises.

Although the mitered designs shown here are all square, these patterns are not limited entirely to this shape. Naturally the square is the best shape, but you can work out a rectangle by lengthening two of the sides and mitering the corners. See page 124. For this shape it is especially interesting to use a line like the one for the last mitered design shown. The background if worked in a continuation of the Florentine stitches will add interest to the center of the piece.

Circular pieces are a little awkward, but if the mitered design itself is carefully chosen and one that has the suggestion of a circular shape, it is possible to work out the background in the round shape and make an attractive piece.

Mitered Bargello is a natural for borders on rugs and pictures, and it is also perfect for use as mirror and picture frames.

Many of the designs in this book can be worked into mitered patterns. The few that are shown are only a beginning. Follow the basic suggestions for working, and plan your own adaptation. This is really fun and is very rewarding since your creation will probably be highly original. This makes the mitered Bargello very exciting. So many possibilities are available that an entire book could be devoted to them—would that we had more space for exploration.

7
BLOCKING

Most of the stitches used in Bargello are upright ones that do not stretch the canvas out of shape, therefore you may be happily surprised to finish your piece and find that it needs very little in the way of blocking. It is always very nice to make this discovery, but, no matter how neat the piece looks, it can be improved with a little blocking. This will often make the difference between the "homemade look" and the "handmade look."

The pieces that are still in their original, straight condition can often be finished with only the application of a little steam. This can be accomplished if the steam iron is used with caution.

To freshen with the steam iron you should lay the Bargello face down on a heavy towel that is placed over an ironing board. Hold the iron just above the surface of the needlepoint and let the steam penetrate the yarn. Do not allow the iron to rest on the needlepoint. This will flatten the stitches and may distort their shape. Leave the steamed piece in position on the board long enough to cool and dry. In many cases you will have a beautifully refreshed piece of Bargello ready for mounting or other finishing.

More often than not, the finished Bargello will be only slightly out of shape but will look rumpled and handled. These pieces really do need more than a simple steaming to make them look new again. To block professionally you will need a blocking board—an old drawing board, bread board, doily blocker, piece of plywood, or builder's composition wallboard will do. You need a clean flat surface into which you do not mind putting a few tack marks. You will also need a supply of rust-proof aluminum or copper tacks. Be certain that these tacks will not rust. Even though you are not going to place them into the finished needlepoint, there is always the possibility that a tack could rust and the rusty water seep along the canvas threads into the yarn, staining it.

Find the center of each border of the Bargello piece and mark these points with a scrap of yarn tied into the canvas. Draw the outline of the finished measurements of the piece on the blocking board. Also mark the centers of the sides on the blocking board. Remember that it is not possible to block out a completed piece of needlepoint to a larger size, therefore the marked size should be that of the original plan.

Wet the needlepoint thoroughly by rolling it in a wet towel and leaving it several hours or overnight. The effect of this method of wetting is to soak equally the yarn and the canvas and make it more amenable to stretching. When the needlepoint is removed from the wet towel it should be very limp. What has happened is that the sizing in the canvas has softened. When dry it will again be crisp and new looking.

Do not wet your needlepoint by holding it under the faucet. That much water is unnecessary and will only lengthen the drying time, and the excess of water will not wet the needlepoint evenly or thoroughly.

Match the marks at the centers of the sides of the Bargello to those on the blocking board. With the needlepoint face up, place a tack at each of these four points. Pull if necessary to make the points match. Working outward from these four points, place a tack about every inch until you have worked around the entire piece. It may be necessary to re-tack some points before you are entirely satisfied that the piece is straight, but the needlepoint will remain wet for several hours—long enough for you to take your time and do a good job. The canvas is a very strong material to which you have added the extra reinforcement of the yarn, thus you also have a very strong fabric that can take the pulling necessary to straighten a stubborn piece.

When the needlepoint has been tacked to the board in a straightened position, it should be left to dry. Care should be taken to dry it in a horizontal position. Do not place in direct sunlight or near heat. Naturally, the weather conditions will affect the drying time, but twenty-four hours is usually sufficient. If the needlepoint feels damp do not remove it from the board because it will revert to its unblocked shape.

There is much discussion about which side of the needlepoint should be down on the board during blocking. Some prefer to place the right side down. This results in the stitches being pressed tightly against the board and does cause some flattening of the stitches. If you prefer this look, do by all means place the needlepoint face down on the blocking board.

8
FINISHING AND MOUNTING

Needlepoint is a very beautiful, heavy fabric and should be considered as such when the time comes to make decisions about finishing and mounting the completed work. If you feel you can do justice to the needlepoint with your sewing skills, you can save a large amount of money by finishing and mounting it yourself. Generally speaking, if the project is one that you would attempt to make up in an expensive and heavy fabric, it will be all right for you to finish in needlepoint. Unfortunately, a skill with the needle in the hands is not always accompanied by a skill with the sewing machine, and beautiful needlepoint can be wasted by clumsy finishing methods. There are many good craftsmen that will take your needlepoint and finish them for you in the manner that these pieces deserve. Very often the price will include blocking, thus saving you that operation also. If you are unsure of yourself you should check into the list of local craftsmen and find someone to help you. If at first the cost of this finishing seems high, consider the lifetime the needlepoint can normally expect. A chair that is upholstered in Bargello may never have to be recovered, slip seats on chairs may never need replacing unless they become excessively soiled, a pillow of Bargello will last longer than the current decorating scheme in a given room.

Some Bargello projects can be finished with only a little basic sewing skill. These are usually the smaller easy to handle items such as pincushions, belts, pillows, book covers, eyeglass cases, doorstops, tote bags, vests, and pictures. Make them up using much the same procedures that you would using a heavy fabric.

A favorite Bargello project is covering slip seats on chairs. If you decide to undertake this, before you start measure your chair seats carefully. Measure from the wood to the wood. Then add one inch to each end of the measurement. Thus if your seat is 18 by 20 inches, the measurements of the finished needlepoint should be 20 by 22 inches. Add two inches on each side for an unworked border, and the dimensions of the canvas you need will be 24 by 26 inches.

Mounting the finished and blocked Bargello is not a tricky job. The only important point is to be sure to pull and tack the Bargello tightly into place. Begin by removing the old upholstery, and replace the padding if necessary. Position the needlepoint on the seat centering the design. Turn the seat over and place a tack in the center of each side. Turn the seat up again and check to be sure the needlepoint has not slipped. Next, tack in place, pulling the needlepoint as tightly as possible. Miter the corners, trimming if necessary to reduce bulk. Cover the entire back of the seat with muslin to enclose the raw edges of the Bargello.

Needlepoint pillows require some sewing skill, but are not difficult to make. They can be made up as either knife-edge pillows or as box pillows, the preference is personal. The fabric used should be of a quality comparable to the needlepoint—a very good quality. Choose the fabric to match the background or to pick up a color from the design.

Muslin-covered pillow forms in standard sizes are available in most needlework departments, which eliminate the need for stuffing the finished pillow with loose filling material. These may be filled with dacron, kapok, or foam rubber, according to your preference.

INDEX